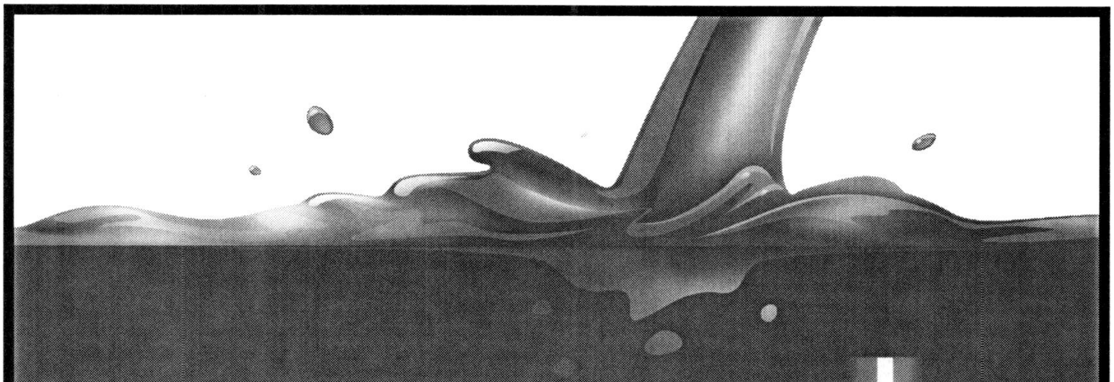

enough

a study on the book of Colossians

crystal colp • jacki kachner • erin lehmann • alice park

Warner Press, Inc
Warner Press and "WP" logo are trademarks of Warner Press, Inc

Enough, A Bible Study on Colossians
Written by Colp, Kachner, Lehmann, and Park

Copyright ©2015 Colp, Kachner, Lehmann, and Park
Cover and layout copyright ©2015 Warner Press Inc

Tree 1:3, an imprint of Warner Press, publishes ministry resources designed to help people grow more deeply in their faith.

Scripture quotations used in this book were taken from the following:
(ESV)—Scripture quotations are from the *ESV® Bible* (*The Holy Bible, English Standard Version®*), copyright © 2001 by Crossway Bibles, a publishing ministry of Good News Publishers. Used by permission. All rights reserved.
(TLB)—Scripture quotations are taken from *The Living Bible* copyright © 1971 by Tyndale House Foundation. Used by permission of Tyndale House Publishers Inc., Carol Stream, Illinois 60188. All rights reserved.
(MSG)—*The Message* (MSG) Copyright © 1993, 1994, 1995, 1996, 2000, 2001, 2002 by Eugene H. Peterson.
(NCV) *The Holy Bible, New Century Version®*. Copyright © 2005 by Thomas Nelson, Inc.
(NIV)—HOLY BIBLE, NEW INTERNATIONAL VERSION®. NIV®. Copyright © 1973, 1978, 1984, 2011 by Biblica, Inc.®. Used by permission. All rights reserved worldwide.
(NIV1984)—Scripture taken from HOLY BIBLE, NEW INTERNATIONAL VERSION®. NIV®. Copyright © 1973, 1978, 1984 by International Bible Society. Used by permission of Zondervan Publishing House. All rights reserved.

All rights reserved. No part of this publication may be reproduced, stored in a retrieval system, or transmitted in any form or by any means—electronic, mechanical, photocopy, recording, or any other—except for brief quotations in printed reviews, without the prior permission of the publisher.

Requests for information should be sent to:
Warner Press Inc
1201 East Fifth Street
P.O. Box 2499
Anderson, IN 46012
www.warnerpress.org

Editor: Karen Rhodes
Cover: Curtis Corzine
Designer: Curtis Corzine

ISBN: 978-1-59317-779-9
E-book ISBN: 978-1-59317-799-7

Printed in USA

Dedicated to our families,
who give us the support, love, and
time necessary to complete a
project like this.

We love you.

Table of Contents

Greetings 6

An Introduction 9

Lesson 1 11

Lesson 2 25

Lesson 3 39

Lesson 4 51

Lesson 5 63

Lesson 6 71

Lesson 7 85

Lesson 8 97

Lesson 9 109

Appendix A–Resources 115

Appendix B–Memory Verses 117

Bibliography 119

Greetings,

Welcome to Colossians! While writing this study we were all weathering interesting situations in our personal lives. It felt at times that we would never see it completed. In the midst of studying this book, however, the one thing that continued to jump out at us was that Christ is enough to see us through whatever we might be going through. So, that became our testimony as we studied Colossians and wrote this for you. What better way to put together a study than to experience the message of it first-hand!

Once again, we have tried to leave room for you to draw your own conclusions about the book of Colossians. Most of the success of this study depends on willing participants, studying together. When you open your books each week, start your time of study with prayer. Ask God to reveal His truth for you that day. As you study allow yourself to be challenged, and be open to new growth as you dig deep in His Word. Remember, our purpose in writing this is not just for the sake of more "knowledge." There is nothing wrong with knowledge, but the key is allowing the knowledge to change you. The purpose is getting to KNOW God's Word so that you can APPLY God's Word.

We would like to give you a few hints for enhancing your study time. As you read Paul's letter to the Colossian people, and learn from it, there may be times that you would like to take further notes or write down more of your thoughts. So, we have included extra note pages at the end of each lesson. Also, a dictionary might come in handy as well. If you are new to Bible Study there may be some words that you would like to look up in order to better understand what you are reading. By the same token, some of us have done a thousand and one Bible studies and we like to skim over words and act like we have an understanding. I encourage you to not rush through and miss out on a blessing. If you are a little unsure of a definition, no one will know if you look it up. Unless you tell them! Be brave ... strive to be a curious student! No one knows it all. Really! In addition to a dictionary, having a copy of the Bible in different versions will give you further insight as you study. We reference *The Message* version of the Bible several times, so this particular one would be especially helpful to you. If you don't already own one, getting this version would be a great purchase; however, it is also easily accessible on the Internet.

In every lesson you will find Deeper Still questions and activities—designed to give those of you who would like to study a little further an opportunity to do so. Do not feel pressured to do them. Just look at these as bonus material. If you have time at the end of your study each week, you can always go back and do these portions. To help with the Deeper Still questions, and any other questions you need further study on, we have included a resource page in the back of the book. We have taken the time to list a few resources that could be helpful in your study time in Colossians, as well as any study you may do of the Bible.

Being able to remember scripture is very beneficial. In those moments when you are in a difficult situation or challenge and you are without your Bible, the Word of God that you have hidden in your heart can be a great comfort. Memorized scripture can also be useful when someone else comes to you with a need. You never know when you might need to call upon the Bible for help. Short of carrying your Bible with you everywhere you go, having verses of it memorized is the only way to be certain that you will have it with you at all times. In an effort to encourage you to keep His Word close, we have included Memory Verses at the beginning of each lesson, with a fill-in-the-blank at the end of each lesson to test your memory! Note that these are the ones that we would suggest you memorize. But, if there is another verse that speaks to your heart from that particular lesson, memorize that one instead! This is just another way of putting this book of the Bible to work in your life!

I wish you could have joined us on the journey of writing this study. We were amazed at how the truth of God's Word came alive in all of our lives as we wrote. Our faith, our prayer lives, and our dependence on the Lord were definitely put to the test during the last few months. Colossians is an inspirational book—a book that reminds you during the toughest of times that Christ is enough. He is all that you need as you navigate the world around you. He is enough to get you through a cancer scare, He is enough to get you through caring for a sick or troubled child, He is enough to get you through an illness, He is enough to give you strength and wisdom as you deal with a struggling household budget, or the loss of a job.

Paul wrote this letter from prison. He was living the testimony that Christ was everything and then some. I pray that as you read and study what God gave us from this letter, you will begin to see Christ as the Supreme One. I pray you will be wary of false teachers and people who would try to lead you astray. Christ has never changed, and He will never change. He is all that you need no matter the circumstances. I cannot wait to hear what happens when you open this tremendous book of the Bible and really get a good look at it. I cannot wait to hear what happens when you begin to apply that Truth to your life. True satisfaction can be yours if you allow Jesus to fill you up with His presence. He is enough!

Satisfied with Jesus,

Crystal Colp

AN INTRODUCTION

The book of Colossians is a letter likely written by the Apostle Paul, probably between 60 and 61 AD. The letter is entitled Colossians simply because it was written to a church in Colossae, a small, seemingly unimportant city located in present-day Turkey in the province of Asia under the Roman Empire. Ironically, Paul may never have visited Colossae. Instead, Epaphras (ee-PAH-fras), who may have become a convert of Paul's during the Apostle's extended ministry in nearby Ephesus, is credited with starting the church in Colossae.

This is thought to have been one of Paul's last letters from prison. Tychicus (TIK-ih-kus), an Asian man who personally visited several churches on Paul's behalf, carried it to the Colossian people. The letter seems to be prompted by the news that the Colossian congregation was allowing false teachings to creep into their community of believers. Epaphras had carefully taught the Gospel and nurtured the converts in the basics of salvation by grace. Young converts, however, were being pressured by advocates of mystical forms of Judaism and pagan ideas. Paul and Epaphras knew if these teachings were not refuted, the converts risked losing their liberty, peace, and joy that Paul knew could only be found in the grace of Jesus Christ.

Paul also sent this letter to us, proclaiming the supremacy and sufficiency of Christ. He emphasizes the completeness that can be found in the unchanging nature of our Savior. Paul's focus makes this letter one of the most Christ-exalted and Christ-centered of all his writings.

> *When I read Paul's letters, I wonder if he had any inkling that we would be reading his words two thousand years later and studying them as guides to faith and God's truth. What a contrast to today's instant messaging and twitter! Most of today's words are hardly relevant for more than a day or two. I am struck by Paul's sensitivity to the situation of his readers and by the great burden he feels for the Colossians, even though he hasn't met them. It is almost as if Paul feels personally responsible to God for each new believer, as*

though he or she were the only one (2 Corinthians 11:28–29). *No man could live like Paul if he were not inspired and empowered by the Spirit of Christ in God. I see in Paul what a life totally lived in Christ Jesus looks like. He inspires me to center my life in Christ.*
—**Alice Park**

Colossians is another writing of Paul's that is completely saturated with the love he feels for its recipients. His desire for them to live a life sold out to Christ is evident in the emotion of his written words. There is no doubt in our minds that the message in Colossians is just as urgent today as it was then, and if Paul were here today he would want you to be a lover of Jesus Christ focused solely on Him! Our prayer, as you work through this study, is that you will get a real sense that Christ is enough for whatever you are facing today or what you will face tomorrow!

deeper still
Using whatever resources you have at your disposal, look up further background information on the church in Colossae. Use the margin or notes page to write down what you find.

before you begin
In order to gain an overview of the entire Book of Colossians, read it from start to finish in one sitting. Don't be intimidated by the word "book." It is very brief—only 4 chapters. Reading the text in several different versions of the Bible can be helpful and can give you greater insight. Use the margins or the notes page to write down your initial thoughts.

Lesson One

Memory Verse:
"here & after repeating. God rescued us from dead-end alleys and dark dungeons. He's set us up in the kingdom of the Son he loves so much, the Son who got us out of the pit we were in, got rid of the sins we were doomed to keep repeating." —Colossians 1:13–14 (*The Message*)

Read Colossians 1:1–14.
Write down your initial thoughts.

_____
_____
_____

Write down any key words you see throughout the text.

_____
_____
_____

From the very beginning of this letter (vs.1) Paul declares to whom he belongs and that his identity is found in being an apostle of Jesus Christ. "Apostle" implies "one who is sent," and in the New Testament church this specifically referred first to the original disciples of Jesus. They were men who had been with Jesus from the beginning of His ministry, witnessed His death, His resurrection, life after resurrection, and ascension. Paul, although converted after Jesus' death, had seen the risen Jesus on the road to Damascus. Now Paul is being careful to present his credentials to the Colossians, who have never met him personally, because he will be asking them to trust what he teaches as the truth rather than the ideas of false teachers who are pressuring them.

Where did Paul receive the confidence and authority to speak as a representative of Christ, finding his identity as an apostle of Jesus? Read the following scriptures to find the answer.

Galatians 1:1–

_____
_____

1 Corinthians 2:1–5–

_____
_____

Acts 9:15–

_____
_____

How would you describe your primary identity?

_____
_____
_____

Where would you say your identity is centered?

_____
_____
_____

Does your identity need some adjusting? Explain.

_____
_____
_____

Our identity is most often found in what our lives are centered around. Paul never writes a letter that leaves the reader guessing where he finds his identity. He wears that truth on his sleeve. And, because of that truth, Paul is largely respected among the New Testament believers. You will never read where Paul uses his identity with Christ to manipulate others or bring honor to himself. He is always careful to give all the glory to God and put the needs of the church at a high priority level. He feels a great amount of responsibility to the church and the preservation of the physical and spiritual health of the body of believers.

Read Colossians 1:2–8. How do you think the people of Colossae felt after hearing these opening remarks?

_____

_____

_____

We will learn later in Colossians that Paul had some very serious concerns about the church at Colossae. He had invested and sacrificed a great deal for the early Christian churches and had earned the right to be heard. Yet, he begins his letter by affirming them and thanking God for them. My guess is they were much more willing to listen to his concerns after he confirmed how much he cared for them. It really does start with the relationship, doesn't it? Have you heard the phrase: "People won't care how much we know until they know how much we care"? Paul totally "got" that concept. The knowledge that they are cared for gives people the ears to hear.

What effect do you think Paul's words of affirmation and thanksgiving for their faith would have had on the Colossians, their self-image, and receptivity to Paul's instructions?

_____

_____

_____

_____

What three Christian virtues in verses 4 & 5 does Paul see in the Colossians that shows him they are true believers in Christ?

_____

_____

_____

_____

What do the following verses say about faith, love, and hope in Christ?

Romans 5:2–5–

_____

_____

_____

1 Corinthians 13:13–

_____

_____

Galatians 5:5–6–

_____

_____

1 Thessalonians 1:3; 5–8–

_____

_____

Hebrews 10:22–24–

_____

_____

What happens when we place our faith, love, and hope in earthly things?

_____

_____

_____

When we have faith, love, and hope in earthly things we can find ourselves in a place of disappointment. The things of this earth are not eternal; however, Jesus is eternal. Jesus stays…forever. And Love and Faith are fruits that can be found in our lives especially when we have a personal, growing relationship with Jesus.

Would you say that you are bearing these fruits in your own life? Explain.

_____

_____

_____

In Colossians 1:5 we read that the fruits of faith and love spring from the hope that is stored up in heaven. **What do you think this means?**

_____

_____

_____

At the end of verse 5 through verse 6, Paul reminds the Colossian people of the truth found in the Gospel of Jesus. He encourages them by telling them of the growth that is happening through that truth all over the world. He takes them back to the day they first heard and understood the message of God's grace. Then in verses 7 and 8 Paul continues to point to the faithfulness of their leader, Epaphras and the way he shared the gospel with them. Paul then lets the Colossians in on the fact that Epaphras is proud of their new-found faith, and he is telling others about the love they had gained through the Spirit.

Paul understood that sometimes being reminded of when your faith began and the circumstances surrounding that moment can bring a renewed sense of purpose. Sometimes we need to get back to the basics—the truth is simple. Paul knew that, and the Colossian people needed a reminder of the simple truth of God's grace in their lives and the love of a leader who was dedicated to teaching them that truth.

Do you remember the day you first heard and understood the Gospel of Jesus? Explain.

_____

_____

_____

_____

Was someone instrumental in leading you to that point? Explain.

_____
_____
_____

When I was 14, my pastor told me to write out my testimony right away. I had just become a Christian and he was excited for me, but also, being wise, knew there would likely come a time when I would doubt my salvation. He wanted me to have proof in my hand when doubts crept in or I questioned my identity in Christ. I still have that handwritten testimony on my school lined paper, written in pencil, and folded like homework. There were a couple times I came across it at just the right time. **—Erin**

Erin's pastor helped her along her faith journey early on. He gave good advice that would help a young Christian find stability in the future. If you are a believer, you have a story to share of how you came to know Christ.

Write out the story of how you became a Christian. *(If you have not accepted Christ as your Savior, this would be a great time to begin your story with Him. If you are ready to take that step today, find a friend or a leader who can pray with you. Or, find a quiet place alone with God and ask Him to forgive you, and accept Him as Lord of your life.)* **If you feel comfortable doing so, come prepared to share your story, your testimony, with the class next week.**

_____
_____
_____
_____
_____

When you accepted Christ or you led someone else to Christ and you began to see growth either in yourself or the other person, you probably wanted to tell others about it. And Epaphras was no different. He told Paul and others about the faith of the Colossian believers.

What do you think others would say of your faith?

_____
_____
_____

Hopefully, you are living out your faith in a way that makes others take note. Even if you are wrestling with some questions in your walk with the Lord, simply living a life of love is one way to share the truth of the gospel with others along the way. Our faith journey can be one that is filled with ups and downs, times of confusion, as well as times of clarity. But, no matter where we are, having prayer support is vitally important. Paul knew this was a must. Paul also goes a step further; he does not just assure the Colossians that he thanks God for their faith and prays for them continually, but he tells them *what* he prays for.

Do you think it is important to be specific in your prayers? Explain.

_____
_____
_____

Do you have something specific you are praying for yourself right now? Are you praying something specific for someone else? If so, write it down. *(If this is confidential, you do not have to share it with the group. It is, however, good to write down specific prayer requests so you can someday go back and see how the Lord answered them.)*

_____
_____
_____

Now go to your text and read verse 9 again. Look at the specifics of Paul's prayer for the Colossian church.

What does Paul say he is asking God to fill them with?

_____
_____
_____

How does Paul say you gain the knowledge of God's will?

_____
_____
_____

How do you think you can have spiritual wisdom and understanding?

_____
_____
_____

Read Psalm 119:97–105. What does this scripture say about gaining understanding? What does it say the word is for our path?

_____
_____
_____

Read Psalm 19:7–11. Remember that law, precepts, statutes, commands, ordinances, etc. are also words used in place of scripture or God's Word. Make a list of the benefits or results of knowing the Word of God. *(example: verse 7—Law of the Lord = revived soul)*

Read 2 Timothy 3:14–15. Where does this scripture say Timothy's wisdom came from?

_____
_____
_____

Deeper Still

Ask someone to be a "Paul" in your life. Ask him or her to become a prayer partner for you, and you for him. Give each other specific requests to pray for each other. Write down his name here, and any specific prayer requests you might give him.

_____

_____

_____

Wisdom, understanding, and growth all come from spending time in God's Word. You are doing just that by being a part of this Bible study. Earlier in verses 5 and 6 Paul spoke of bearing fruit. The fruit you bear in your life is a direct result of where you plant yourself. Planting yourself in the Word of God enables you to live a life worthy of the Lord, and that is pleasing to Him.

What do you think "living a life worthy of the Lord" looks like?

_____

_____

_____

Paul really breaks down the subject of living a worthy life for us. In verse 10 through the beginning of verse 12, he lists several things we can do in order to live a life pleasing to God. **Make a list of these things in the space provided below.**

_____

_____

_____

Paul knew what they needed to walk their path in life here on earth. He knew what it would take to live a life worthy of the eternal gifts and the Giver of those matchless gifts. Praying specifically for them to gain these necessities was of utmost importance to him.

Paul's prayer (vs.9–12) is one of my favorite prayers in the Bible. I often pray it for others and for myself because I know there is no greater fulfillment and joy than doing God's glorious will and being who He created us to be for Him. Yet it isn't an easy prayer. It is a prayer of total surrender of my new self each day to Jesus to be His body in this world. If I hesitate because I am afraid of giving up what pleases me or others, or if I am afraid God will ask me to suffer, my heart is divided and I have no peace. I must look again to the cross where I was crucified with Jesus. There I see once again that there is nothing, no life for me apart from Jesus. How awful then to desire anything but to please the loving Master who gives His life and every good thing to me. And what joy and peace transform the most common of days when I know I am where He wants me to be. I can rest in the yoke of Jesus, trusting Him to bear the responsibility for my outcomes and to supply the strength I need to obey Him. **—Alice**

Paul prayed for what the Colossian people would need to be strong and to live a life of obedience, even when they were being bombarded with untruths. And, after telling them in detail what he is praying for them, Paul decides that this group of people also needs to be reminded of one more very important thing. He reminds them of what God, the Father, has done for them. I can almost hear the urgency and concern in his voice as he gently nudges them to keep the main thing the main thing! He is concerned that their eyes are being turned away from the one true God. He is trying to draw them back to the truth that would point them in the direction of their Savior.

Read verses 12–14. What does Paul say that God has done for them?

_____

_____

_____

This was not just done for the Colossian people. God did this for all believers. He has done this for us…for you. He rescued us. Set us free. He gave us an inheritance that we do not deserve. Most days I need to be reminded of this truth. And the way to remember is to spend time in the Word of God. When I am in His Word, I am abiding in Him. I pray that you are abiding in Him and His Word. I so long for you to see past the junk the world is throwing at you today to see the truth of His grace and love for you. Paul's heart was for this body of believers to find freedom in salvation, bringing the hope of eternity, and God's heart is the same for you.

Do you sense that hope in your life? If so, explain. If not, write a specific prayer asking that God, the Father, would open a spring of new hope in your life today.

_____
_____
_____
_____
_____

We have looked at the first 14 verses of Paul's letter to the Colossians. We have already learned quite a bit from his words to this group of people, and we have much more to look at. There is, however, one very important question that must be asked before we proceed: Do you know Him as your personal Lord and Savior? If you have never accepted Him as your Savior and you would like to do so, ask your leader to pray with you. There is no time like the present. Please do not put it off one more day. We would love to celebrate that decision with you.

If you do know Him as your Savior, then celebrate today the hope that you have in Him. Paul's letter is a great encouragement for believers to remember what He gave for us. If you have a "To Do" list, then write this on it: REMEMBER TO LIVE IN HOPE! That hope should draw you to His Word. His Word should bring about growth and wisdom, which should inspire you to love. And that love WILL draw others to Him!

_____
_____
_____
_____
_____

In Summary
Now take some time to go through the text once more (Colossians 1:1–14). After studying a little deeper, what did you learn? How can you apply that to your own life?

1:1–2– _____
_____

1:3–4– _____
_____

1:5–8– _____
_____

1:9–11– _____
_____

1:12–14– _____
_____

Application
This week look for an opportunity to live out the hope you have in Christ by loving on others. Look for a simple way to just show love. Maybe you can love your waitress at the restaurant by giving an extra large tip, maybe a neighbor could use dinner, or the person in line behind you in the drive-thru would find it amazing that you bought their coffee anonymously. Whatever you choose to do, write it down here and share what you did next week with the group.

_____
_____
_____
_____
_____
_____

Memory Verse Review:

"God _____ us from dead-end alleys and _____.

He's set us up in the _____ of the _____

He loves so much, the Son who got us _____ of the

_____ we were in, got rid of the _____ we were

_____ to keep repeating."

         Colossians 1:_____ (The Message)

Notes:

LESSON TWO

Memory Verse:
"For by him all things were created, in heaven and on earth, visible and invisible, whether thrones or dominions or rulers or authorities—all things were created through him and for him. And he is before all things, and in Him all things hold together." —Colossians 1:16–17 (ESV)

Read Colossians 1:15–23.
Write down your initial thoughts.

_____
_____
_____

Write down any key words you see throughout the text.

_____
_____
_____

Before we get into the text too far, answer the following questions:

When you picture God, what comes to mind?

_____
_____

When you picture Jesus, what comes to mind??

_____
_____

These might seem like difficult questions. The reason these might be difficult questions is found in verse 15. And that is, He is invisible. God might be the most difficult Pictionary clue ever! It is very difficult to try to picture someone who has never been seen, so all of us probably answered these questions in very different ways. The clue to knowing who God is lies in knowing who Jesus is. Verse 15 says, *He is the image of the invisible God....* The word "image" implies exact likeness. Christ came so that men could see the true God, just as Christ saw the Father in the heavenly realm. When you spend time in God's Word getting to know Jesus, you are getting to know God and developing an image of Who God the Father is.

What do the following verses teach us about seeing God?

John 14:8–10–

_____
_____
_____

Hebrews 1:2–3–

_____
_____
_____

At times it is very difficult to continually relate and feel close to God, because we cannot hear or see Him in the physical sense.

> *The thought struck me as I read verse 15 in* The Message: *"We look at this Son and see the God who cannot be seen." Wouldn't we just love to feel and touch God? Wouldn't it be great if we could actually see Him walking beside us? It's said there is power in numbers, and I personally would feel pretty powerful...almost like Super Woman...if God's physical presence was with me. And let's face it there are times in our lives when God seems particularly silent and we really wonder if He even knows our name or cares about the pressing issues in our lives. As I was contemplating this scenario I got to thinking about all the things I never see that exist in my life. How about electricity for example? Each month I faithfully pay my bill even though I never actually see electricity. Sure, I see the results of the electrical current running into my home, powering all of my electrical appliances. I see the impact it has on my life. I believe it exists. Without it I would be, quite literally, in the dark. And when it goes out, I go nuts...no lights, no microwave,*

no computer…it is not good. I have come to depend on it in so many ways. It is the same scenario with God. We can't see Him but we can look for all the ways He has impacted our lives. The evidence of His existence is everywhere…in a rainbow, in the air we breathe, in the flowers we enjoy, and most especially in the gift of His Son, Jesus, and the hope of eternity. —Jacki

In what ways is it difficult for you to relate to an invisible God you cannot see?

_____

_____

_____

How does knowing Jesus help with these difficulties?

_____

_____

_____

How can you "see" Jesus more accurately or get to know Him more intimately?

_____

_____

_____

The major key to knowing God is to know His Son. We can get to know Jesus better when we truly understand His supremacy. Verses 15 through 20 speak to that subject.

Read verses 15–20 again, and list the ways that Christ is supreme:

Supreme in creation:

Vs 15– _____
_____
_____

Vs 16– _____
_____
_____

Vs 17– _____
_____
_____

Supremacy in redemption:

Vs 18– _____
_____

Vs 19 & 20– _____
_____

Why do you think Paul listed all of these attributes of God?
_____
_____
_____

The false teachers in Colossae, like many people today, had differing ideas about Christ. They taught that special intellectual knowledge and legalism, in addition to Christ, were necessary for spiritual completeness. In this entire portion of Scripture, Paul gives a defense of the key claim of the Christian faith: knowing and being obedient to Jesus Christ as our Savior are necessary to experience God fully. Paul writes in poetic form, which suggests to some scholars that these verses were part of an early Christian hymn of praise. In any case, this passage is all about Jesus; pronouns refer to Him in every verse. The Colossian people were being led astray with false doctrine, perhaps even false teachings about God as the Creator, so it is not surprising that Paul would take the opportunity to write about this subject. He begins this line of thinking at the end of verse 15, using the terminology of Jesus being "the firstborn over all creation." Firstborn in this context means honored or most-favored. In essence, Jesus is the chosen Son of God, honored and most-favored above all else. He has always been by God the Father's side. So, Jesus was there from the beginning—when every living thing was created. Paul is once again reminding the Colossian people of a truth they should know: Jesus is the Son of God, the Creator of the universe, and the most honored firstborn over all others.

Read John 1:1–3. In this portion of Scripture Jesus is "The Word." What information do you learn about Jesus from this portion of Scripture?

_____

_____

_____

Write down how you find this truth repeated in these verses:

Hebrews 1:2–

_____

_____

1 Corinthian 8:6–

_____

_____

1 John 1:1–3–

_____

_____

Look at the end of Colossians 1:16 again. What or who was everything created for?

_____

_____

If everything was created for Him, then how should that affect our personal goals and aspirations?

_____

_____

_____

How is that fact being reflected or not reflected in your life right now?

_____

_____

_____

When I think of "all things being created for Him" that seems to take the pressure off. What I mean is: it takes the pressure off of trying to please people, of trying to find success just to keep up with the Joneses. It means that any success that comes is for His glory, any pleasing to be done should be for Him, and the way I view what is important takes on a whole new look. Likewise, when things feel like they are falling apart, it is to Him I should turn. Verse 17 is probably one of my favorite verses in this section of Scripture. The Message puts it this way: "He was there before any of it came into existence and (He) holds it all together right up to this moment." When I am looking at a situation in my life that seems to be falling apart at the seams, I need to remember He is in control. He has a heavenly view of the situation. Not only is He holding that situation together, but He is holding me together too. At the end of the day He should be enough! One of my favorite songs says it better than I ever could. It is a song called "Enough" by Chris Tomlin:

All of You is more than enough for all of me
For every thirst and every need
You satisfy me with Your love
And all I have in You is more than enough.

*You're my supply my breath of life
Still more awesome than I know
You're my reward worth living for
Still more awesome than I know.*

*All of You is more than enough for all of me,
For every thirst and every need.
You satisfy me with Your love,
And all I have in You is more than enough.*

*You're my sacrifice of greatest price
Still more awesome than I know
You're my coming King You are ev'rything
Still more awesome than I know*

*More than all I want more than all I need
You are more than enough for me
More than all I know more than all I can say
You are more than enough*[1]

I guess that pretty much says it all. No matter what comes my way or your way He truly is enough.
—Crystal

The Colossian people were being led astray by false teachers who were telling them Jesus was not enough and not that special after all. They were being taught they had to engage in worshiping these other angels and involve themselves in following a set of legalistic rules. Paul wanted them to understand in no uncertain terms that JESUS is sovereign. In the dictionary *sovereign* literally means: independent of the control of others. He doesn't need help…HE is all you need.

Do you believe Jesus is enough just as He is?

_____
_____
_____

Paul carries verse 16 right into verse 17, connecting the two verses by using the word *and*. He is saying: not only is He holding it all together, He is also the head of the church, the beginning, and the firstborn among the dead. I don't know what you think, but that is one huge job description. But I guess if the job is RULER OF THE UNIVERSE (Can you hear your voice echoing as you say that?), I guess this list of expectations is nothing to shy away from! Paul wants these people to get the picture already. He wants to stir up in them the boldness, confidence, and unwavering faith that comes from serving the great and awesome God.

When Paul says, "He is the head of the body, the church," that word *church* includes all believers who are saved by grace through faith in Jesus. He is linking the Colossians to all Christians everywhere and in every time, beyond their particular congregation. Jesus is the natural head, ruler, protector, and unifier of all believers as the first to be resurrected to immortality, and the agent by which we all will be resurrected one day.

How do you honor Jesus as the head in your relationships and interactions with others?

_____

_____

_____

Can a Christian fulfill Jesus' personal purpose for her/his life apart from other believers? Explain.

_____

_____

_____

_____

What do the following scriptures say about being a member of the body of Jesus, the Church?

Romans 12:4–5–

_____

_____

_____

1 Corinthians 12:12–27–

_____

_____

_____

Being a part of the body of Christ, the Church, can be a tremendous source of strength for the individual believer. That strength comes from the spiritual unity found within the common bond of loving and serving Jesus. But, Jesus paid a high price for us and for the Church. That price was death on the cross. Ultimately He was resurrected, and now He has supremacy. He conquered death and is supreme over all. In *The Message*, Colossians 1:18 & 19 says, *"He was supreme in the beginning and leading the resurrection parade—He is supreme in the end. From the beginning to the end He's there, towering far above everything, everyone. So spacious is He, so roomy, that everything of God finds its proper place in Him without crowding."*

> *So Christ is the Grand Marshall, leading the parade! Who among us has not watched the Rose Parade on New Year's Day? Don't we wonder who the Grand Marshall will be? It is usually someone we admire or at the very least, a well-known celebrity. (I attended the Rose Parade in 2010 and the GM was Chesley Sullenberger, the pilot who landed an airplane in the Hudson River. In 2011 the GM was Paula Dean; I believe her claim to fame is tied to the butter industry!) As the Grand Marshall approaches, people stretch their necks and hush their children in eager anticipation of his/her arrival. They want to see the Grand Marshall clearly and oooh and ahhh as their float passes by. That's where God wants to be in our lives…leading our parade, leading our lives, and leading us to a life of holiness, set apart from the things of this world.*
> *—Jacki*

He wants that supreme, first place position in our lives. This takes us to a place in our time of study that warrants some self-evaluation.

Take a minute to evaluate your life and your priorities. Is Jesus supreme in your life? Does He have first place? Explain.

_____

_____

_____

_____

If you answered, "No, Jesus does not have first place in my life" to the previous question, then explain what takes priority over Him? How do you think you could change that?

_____

_____

_____

_____

Jesus not only needs to have that position in your life, He deserves it because He earned the right. You see, since the fall of man in the Garden of Eden, man has lost his spiritual connection. Before Adam's sin, God and man were together in harmony, in agreement. Adam, not God, broke that agreement. We have turned away from God to live for ourselves. Because of this, there is an ongoing battle for our souls. Jesus fought the greatest spiritual battle in history to gain for us the right to choose salvation. The cross was a pivotal moment in human history. God could once again live in communion with His people.

Read verse 19 again. How did God feel about doing this for us?

_____

_____

_____

_____

God sacrificed His Son. God paid the price with the blood of His Son. And the scripture said He was pleased to do so. Pleased? Not begrudging? He loves us THAT much. He knew the ultimate reward. He could see past the cross to what was beyond the death and burial. He knew that without the cross there would be no salvation.

Read Hebrews 9:22. What had to happen for forgiveness of sin to be possible?

_____

_____

Now read Colossians 1:20. How was peace made?

_____

_____

_____

Now that we have the *knowledge* of the cross and the peace that was made there, how do we *apply* it? We must act upon that knowledge and accept the grace that is being offered. We know this and so did Paul. He wanted that desperately for the Colossian people. He wanted them to understand that Jesus did EVERYTHING that was necessary. Accepting Him and His salvation was all that was necessary on their part. Again, Paul wanted them and us to understand that Jesus is enough, and these false teachers with their addendums to the gospel story are FALSE teachers. So, Paul decided to make his plea a bit more personal. In verses 21-23 of our text Paul turns from the general to the personal *you*. This applies the truth of the cross and the salvation found there to the Colossian believers and even to us today!

Looking at verses 21–23, how does Paul describe the past spiritual condition of the Colossians?

_____

_____

_____

How does Paul describe their present spiritual condition in Jesus, though imperfect?

_____
_____
_____

How does he describe their future spiritual experience and fulfillment in Jesus?

_____
_____
_____

Paul is trying to take the Colossian people and us past the *what* of the cross, past the experience of it. He wants us to focus our direct attention on the *who* of the cross—to focus on Jesus and find a personal walk with Him—a personal walk. He does this by once again using this letter as a reminder. He brings it all to fruition by taking them back to what their future is, "IF" they continue in their faith (vs 1:23). He did this in Colossians 1:13-14 also.

Go back to last week's lesson and read verses 13 & 14 of last week's text. What did God do for us?

_____
_____
_____

What do we have through His Son?

_____
_____
_____

Paul is repeating himself in the same chapter, and he is not just doing it for fun. He is doing it to make sure they remember. He is doing it, not because he doubts their dedication to Jesus. In fact in verse 23, the opening phrase in the Greek indicates that Paul is not expecting the Colossians to deny Jesus. You can also translate the word "if" to "since" instead. So, this verse could just as well say, "Since you continue in your faith." He has no doubt that they will remain faithful to Him. But, like the parable Jesus told of the two builders, Paul is stressing the importance of remaining faithful by building their faith on a solid foundation of truth, and not the shifting sands of the false teachers. In essence, he is encouraging the Colossian people to keep on keeping on. Paul wants them to remember the gift and hang on to it. He wants them to remember the truth of the gospel—to understand once and for all that Jesus Christ is THE TRUTH. His desire is for the Colossian people to remain faithful, firm, and unmoved from the living and lasting hope that is held within the person of Jesus, for He truly is enough!

In Summary
Now take some time to go through the text (Colossians 1:15–23) once more. After studying a little deeper, what did you learn? How can you apply that to your own life?

1:15–17– _____

_____

1:18–20– _____

_____

1:21–22– _____

_____

1:23– _____

_____

Application

As we have studied together this week, there have undoubtedly been some burdens you feel like you have been trying to carry alone...things you have not turned over completely to Jesus. In essence, you have doubted that He is enough to help you with whatever load you're carrying. We all have moments in our lives when we feel hopeless. I pray that you have been reminded of the hope that is found in Jesus. I pray you are at a place where you are willing to allow Jesus to take control and to be your all in all. If you would like to give your burdens to Him, take a few moments to place the load you are carrying at His feet. In the space below, draw the outline of a cross. Now write along the lines of the cross the burdens you are carrying alone. Write in what is weighing you down. Turn them over to Him and live in the new assurance that He is enough for you!

Memory Verse:

"For in _____ all things were _____:

things in _____ and on _____,

_____ and _____, whether _____

or _____ or _____ or _____;

all things have been_____ through Him and for

_____. He is _____ all things, and in him all

things hold _____."

Colossians 1:16–17 (NIV)

[1] Copyright © 2002 worshiptogether.com Songs (ASCAP) sixsteps Music (ASCAP) (adm. at CapitolCMGPublishing.com) All rights reserved. Used by permission.

Lesson Three

Memory Verse:
"The mystery in a nutshell is just this: Christ is in you, so therefore you can look forward to sharing in God's glory. It's that simple. That is the substance of our Message."   —Colossians 1:27 (*The Message*)

Read Colossians 1:24—2:5.
Write down your initial thoughts.

_____
_____
_____

Write down any key words you see throughout the text.

_____
_____
_____

Paul suffered because he was spreading the gospel. He was persecuted on a daily basis because of his love for Jesus and his dedication to seeing that everyone heard the good news of the gospel. Most of us have never really had to suffer for Jesus. But I am sure you can recall a time in your life when you were suffering either mentally, emotionally, physically, spiritually, or in some other way. During that time I doubt that you would have ever said as Paul did, "I rejoice in what was suffered." In Max Lucado's book *Walking with the Savior*, he echoes Psalm 34:1–2 when he writes:

> We should serve God even if there is darkness enveloping our life
>   I will praise the Lord at all times;
> And even if we don't understand what's happening...
>   His praise is always on my lips.
> Even when the circumstances of our life don't make sense:
>   My whole being praises the Lord.
> Because he is worthy of praise, because He is God.[1]

Have you ever had a time where it felt like darkness was enveloping your life? If so, explain. (If not, have you ever helped a friend or loved one walk through a dark time in their lives? Explain.)

_____
_____
_____

How did you feel during that time?

_____
_____
_____

How would you rate your relationship with God before that experience? How about during that experience? And after that experience?

_____
_____
_____

Most of us would not say that we were happy during a dark time in our lives. As a matter of fact, we would probably say that we were miserable. Paul was different. He rejoiced.

Why do you think Paul was happy in his suffering?

_____
_____
_____

We were never promised that life would be all rainbows and roses. We were never promised that we would not suffer. Individuals all across our world suffer for the cause of Christ. Such suffering and hardship can occur in all kinds of ways and to all different degrees. Paul understood that sometimes suffering is necessary to advance the gospel. Paul wrote this letter from the prison in Rome—put there because of his belief in Jesus as the Christ and his ministry to share that with whomever he came in contact. Paul was experiencing suffering at a high degree. His life and ministry during these times of suffering had a profound impact on many people then and now.

Look up the following verses and write down what they have to say about suffering:

John 15:18–21–

_____

_____

2 Timothy 1:8–9–

_____

_____

_____

2 Timothy 2:8–13–

_____

_____

_____

2 Corinthians 4:8–11–

_____

_____

_____

Galatians 2:20–

_____

_____

_____

Paul knew that suffering came as a result of the job he had to do as a part of the kingdom of God. In verse 25 of our text he indicates that God had given him a special job to do, and that was to share the truth of Jesus with everyone he could. He was to enhance and expand the growing reputation of Jesus as the Savior.

Have you ever met someone that thoroughly enhanced the reputation of Jesus for you and perhaps for others? If so, explain.

_____
_____
_____

How did their commitment affect you?

_____
_____
_____

I am sure that the Colossian people were overwhelmingly changed by the life and ministry of Paul. His commitment to Jesus and to them was so strong that not even prison could stop him from ministering to the people he was called to love and serve. As we continue to look at verse 25, you will notice that Paul uses the phrase "fully tell." Scholars believe that to fully present the gospel means to proclaim it to those who have not heard. In other words, it is not enough to just KNOW the gospel; we also need to TELL the gospel.

Deeper Still

Romans 15:19 also uses the term "fully." Read this verse and note any further insight it provides.

If you notice in that same verse (25) he calls himself a "servant." In Colossians 1:1 he refers to himself as an apostle, and now he describes himself as a servant. This is indicative of the responsibility he feels toward the Colossian people. In the Greek this word means, "the management of a household; specifically the oversight and administration of another's property." God had entrusted him with the gospel message, and he felt as personally responsible to seeing it spread throughout the world as a servant would feel responsible to administrate his owner's property faithfully.

Do you consider yourself a servant of Jesus? If so, explain.

_____
_____
_____

Do you think we all have a responsibility as servants of Jesus Christ to not only know the word of God but to also share it with others? Explain.

_____
_____
_____

Pastors preach sermons. Some people choose to hand out tracts. But, there are other ways to share the message of Jesus with others. What are some other ways we can TELL others about Jesus?

_____
_____
_____

How do you TELL others about Jesus and the hope you have in Him?

_____
_____
_____

Verse 27 sums it all up: Paul had a message to share, a job to do. His main desire and focus was to TELL the world the gospel message. And, "*the essence of that message...is this: Christ is the Head of the universe. We approach Him directly, not through intermediary angels. He, not this or that philosophy, or this or that set of rules, but Christ Himself is our Wisdom, our Life, our Hope of Glory.*"[2] Some translations use the word *"mystery"* to describe the message of Christ in verse 26 and two other times in this section. It puzzles many people because today we use "mystery" to mean something we can't ever understand or know. In the New Testament it designates something we can't humanly know but that God reveals to man.

So His whole purpose for mankind through Christ is even more awesome and a matter of faith because only God can reveal it (see also Hebrews 1:1–3). Christ is ENOUGH! Paul could not contain his love of Jesus Christ. He could not keep silent about this mystery any longer.

Read Colossians 1:28. (If possible read this portion of Scripture in a couple other translations to help you see the full meaning.) Why does Paul say we should proclaim Jesus?

_____

_____

_____

That verse also says we should admonish and teach with all wisdom. What does the word _admonish_ mean to you?

_____

_____

_____

When we allow someone to hold us accountable, it means she needs to "hold our feet to the fire." In other words, there may be times when the person has to let us know in a loving way that we are off track! I want people in my life who are full of the wisdom that comes from a growing relationship with Jesus Christ to keep me grounded. I want friends who not always just tell me what I want to hear, but will instead say the hard things at times when I need it. Without those kinds of people in my life, my walk with the Lord could be very different today. I believe that is what Paul was trying his very best to be in the lives of the Colossian people. Out of love for these people, he was admonishing and teaching because he wanted them to have a vibrant faith that was not easily led astray.

Do you have a "Paul" in your life, someone to hold you accountable, to admonish and teach you when you need it? Explain.

_____

_____

_____

Have you ever been that person for someone else? Explain.

_____

_____

_____

What effect do these types of relationships have on your walk with the Lord?

_____

_____

_____

It takes work to have mature, honest relationships with others. It takes spending time with one another and being real—leaving our egos at the door. It takes humility and vulnerability to allow people in to that degree. Paul worked hard to be an open book when it came to his struggles, his faith, and his ministry. He was open with his congregations so they could feel safe and open with him. In 1:29, Paul talks about what it takes for him to maintain this level of intimacy with others. In order for him to proclaim Christ, he needs strength.

Where does Paul say that his strength comes from?

_____

_____

_____

Read verses 28 & 29 aloud. What end is Paul struggling and laboring for?

_____

_____

_____

How should Paul's example affect us in terms of how we labor and struggle in our own lives?

_____

_____

_____

Paul was not just struggling over things in his own life. He was laboring for people he had never even met. And he was doing so because he believed he had a purpose.

Read Colossians 2:1–3. What was Paul's purpose in struggling for people he had never met?

_____

_____

_____

Verse 2 in *The Message* says this: "*I want you woven into a tapestry of love, in touch with everything there is to know about God.*"

The word tapestry really caught my attention, and I spent some time reading about how tapestries were created centuries ago. First of all, they were intended to tell or create a story. It would take months and often years to create the finished product. Besides being beautiful they also had many practical uses. They could provide insulation for castle walls, cover openings, and offer privacy around beds.

> *I think it is important to remember that being woven as an individual in Christ usually takes a lifetime. God can take anyone and turn him or her into a beautiful tapestry as long as his or her hearts are open and willing to receive His message. Along with being beautifully created to serve Him, we also need to weave love along our path in life. All around us are hurting people who do not feel accepted, loved, safe, and certainly not beautiful. Maybe you are one of them. But God, through His Son, wants to create a deeply woven tapestry in you that will last forever.* **–Jacki**

As God is weaving our lives into beautiful tapestries, we encounter moments with Christ that bring clarity to our purpose in life. The mystery of who He is and how He is at work in our lives begins to open up little by little. In verse 3, Paul says wisdom and knowledge are hidden treasures that are found within Christ. Paul goes on in verse 4 to tell them that if they will seek out these hidden treasures they will not be easily deceived.

How do you think we can find the hidden treasures of wisdom and knowledge?

_____

_____

_____

I don't believe that one person can have all there is to have when it comes to these treasures. I believe it is a process…a journey…of unraveling the mystery and the treasures that only Christ and the study of His Word can bring to our lives. It is only when we see him face-to-face that the treasures are gained to their fullest. That is when the treasure hunt ends. While we are still living here on earth, we should always be striving to gain more and more wisdom and understanding. When someone believes he or she knows all there is to know of Christ then there could be an ego problem, a stagnation problem, a stubbornness issue, or a failure to place priority on knowing more of Him. I pray that you are not there. I pray that you have an overwhelming desire to be on a treasure hunt for more of Him every day of your life so you cannot be deceived. This will bring about the firm faith that Paul talks about in Colossians 1:5.

If you look at verse 2:5 in *The Message*, Paul says that he *is* "impressed with the solid substance of their faith in Christ."

In your own words what do the following scriptures say about a solid foundation?

Isaiah 28:16–

_____

_____

_____

Luke 6:46–49–

_____
_____
_____

2 Timothy 2:19–

_____
_____
_____

Why is it important to have a solid foundation of our faith?

_____
_____
_____

There is an old hymn entitled "The Solid Rock" by William Bradbury. This hymn speaks of the ageless truth that Jesus is the only firm foundation upon which to stand:

> *My hope is built on nothing less*
> *Than Jesus' blood and righteousness;*
> *I dare not trust the sweetest frame,*
> *But wholly lean on Jesus' name.*
>
> *On Christ the solid Rock, I stand;*
> *All other ground is sinking sand,*
> *All other ground is sinking sand.*

Are you standing on Christ? Do you feel like your foundation is solid and firm? Explain.

_____
_____
_____

This week I pray that you will unravel more and more of the treasures God has for you in His Word. If you could not answer that Christ is your own personal solid foundation, I pray that you will seek the strength, the wisdom, and the understanding to begin to build that strong foundation on Him, a priceless treasure. All of Him is way more than enough for you to stand upon!

_____
_____
_____

In Summary
Now take some time to go through the text once more (Colossians 1:24—2:5). After studying a little deeper, what did you learn? How can you apply that to your own life?

1:24–27– _____
_____
_____

1:28–29– _____
_____
_____

2:1–3– _____
_____
_____

2:4–5– _____
_____
_____

Application

Make a commitment to join the treasure hunt for wisdom and understanding. One way to do this would be to set aside a time everyday to spend in the Word of God and in prayer. You may choose to read a portion of Scripture and journal your thoughts, do a Bible study like this one, or use any number of other resources that have you reading at least a verse from the Bible consistently. Keeping a prayer journal is also a way to keep track of the way God is revealing Himself to you. Write down in the space provided what your plan is going to be in order to stay in the hunt! Then write a prayer of commitment, asking the Lord to grant you the strength to continue laboring for Him.

Memory Verse:

"The _____ in a nutshell is just this: _____ is in you, so therefore you can look _____ to sharing in God's _____. It's that _____. That is the _____ of our _____."

Colossians 1:_____ (*The Message*)

---

[1] Max Lucado, *Walking with the Savior*, (Wheaton: Tyndale, 1996), 102.
[2] Henry H. Halley, *Halley's Bible Handbook*, (Grand Rapids: Zondervan, 1961), 622.

Lesson Four

Memory Verse:
"For God was pleased to have all his fullness dwell in Him, and through Him to reconcile to Himself all things, whether things on earth or things in heaven, by making peace through his blood, shed on the cross."

—Colossians 1:19–20 (NIV)

Read Colossians 2:6–15
Write down your initial thoughts.

_____
_____
_____

Write down any key words you see throughout the text.

_____
_____
_____

In verse 6, *so then* signals a hinge in Paul's thought—joining the teaching before with the logical outcome. Paul has presented to the Colossians the real truth about Christ: the mystery that He dwells within the heart of all believers as they have faith in Him and the Church, as his visible body on earth. He places the believers firmly in Christ before he attacks the false teachings. The false teachers were saying that if you wanted to gain God completely, it was not enough to just belong to Christ. But we know that the opposite of that is true. Christ is enough, and that is the TRUTH! As you read verse 6, notice that the word *received* is past tense. The Colossian people had accepted Christ and His teachings already. Paul is trying His best to remind them of this.

Read verse 6 again. What do you think it means to *receive Christ as Lord*?

_____

_____

_____

Do you think that the relationship begins and ends at the point when we accept Him as Lord, or is it a growing relationship that we experience in new ways as our life changes and our understanding of Christ expands? Explain from your own experience.

_____

_____

_____

Read the following verses and record what you learn about Jesus Christ as Lord:

Matthew 7:21–

_____

_____

_____

Romans 10:9, 10:12–13 –

_____

_____

_____

Romans 14:8–9–

_____

_____

_____

Philippians 2:9–11–

_____

_____

_____

Paul reminds them who is Lord in their lives, then encourages them to *continue to live in Him*. He goes on to explain what that means in verse 7. He lists 4 keys to living in Christ: rooted in Him, built up in Him, strengthened in faith, and overflowing with thankfulness.

In your own words, what do these 4 keys look like?

Rooted in Him–

_____

_____

_____

Built up in Him–

_____

_____

_____

Strengthened in faith–

_____

_____

_____

Overflowing with thankfulness–

_____

_____

_____

Paul obviously thought that these 4 things were important steps in the lives of the Colossian people and their relationship with Christ. They are just as important for us today. Take a deeper look at these keys to growth.

The idea of being rooted is referenced many times in the Bible. Read the following verses and reflect on what it means to be connected to and rooted in Christ:
Psalm 92:12–15–

_____

_____

_____

Jeremiah 17:7–8–

_____

_____

_____

John 15:5–8–

_____

_____

_____

Ephesians 3:16–19–

_____

_____

_____

Deeper Still

Use whatever resources you have at your disposal. Look up other verses that refer to this idea of being rooted in Christ. List them in the space provided.

_____

_____

_____

In your opinion, what is the difference in being rooted in Christ and built on Christ?

_____

_____

_____

Read Luke 6:46–49. How can you apply this parable to your own life?

_____

_____

_____

Read the following scriptures and respond by answering the question: What foundation must we always be building our faith upon so that we can stand firm and at peace through all the storms and tests of this life?

1 Corinthians 3:9–11–

_____

_____

_____

Ephesians 2:20–22–

_____

_____

_____

1 Peter 2:4–6–

_____

_____

_____

In most of Paul's writing he refers to the source of his strength being outside of himself. As a matter of fact, he has already referred to this in Colossians.

Read Colossians 1:29. What or who is the source of Paul's strength?

_____
_____
_____

Are you stronger when you are rooted and built on Christ? Explain.

_____
_____
_____

How strong do you feel today? If you feel weak, why do you think that is? If you feel strong, explain your source of strength.

_____
_____
_____

Remembering what we have to be thankful for brings strength, peace, and comfort to our lives. Paul was a man who dwelled in thankfulness. He knew that nothing was greater than the gift of salvation through Jesus Christ, and that was enough. When he was in prison, he could be thankful. When he was beaten, he could be thankful. When he was shipwrecked, he could be thankful. No matter the circumstances in his life, he always had something to be thankful for, and that brought resilience and strength to him in the darkest times. He had a true understanding of God's grace, and that produced joy and gratitude in his heart. The cross was for Paul and it was for you. That is something to be thankful for even when you feel like there is nothing else good going on in your life. You were loved enough to die for. Gratitude should spring and flow from that point to then include other gifts God has given in your life.

Write down what you are thankful for.

_____
_____
_____
_____

Is your level of gratitude rising as you learn more and more about God's love for you? Explain.

_____
_____
_____

In *The Message,* verses 6–7 say: *"My counsel for you is simple and straight-forward: Just go ahead with what you've been given. You received Christ Jesus, the Master; now live Him. You're deeply rooted in Him. You're well constructed upon Him. You know your way around the faith. Now do what you've been taught. School's out; quit studying the subject and start living it! And let your living spill over into thanksgiving."* In essence Paul is trying to get them to a point of application. He wants them to live what they have been taught, not to be distracted by false teaching. He wants them to live it so they can become stronger. And that is what we should do…apply the Word of God to our lives. We can start that right now!

How do you think you could begin to apply these 4 keys to growth in your own life? Do you struggle with applying any one of these keys? Explain.

_____
_____
_____
_____

Living out your faith along with consistent growth in your relationship with Christ is needed in order to steer clear of deception that the world will throw at you as you walk through life. Every day there are new temptations and every day we must be prepared to meet them head on with the truth of God's Word. In verse 8 of our text, Paul warns the Colossian people to beware of *"hollow and deceptive philosophy, which depends on human tradition and basic principles of this world."* He warns them to not be taken captive by any such thing. The only way to prevent that captivity is to test what comes against us with the truth of Jesus Christ.

What are some of the empty and deceptive philosophies that tempt people today? What makes them so appealing?

_____

_____

_____

_____

The Colossian people were being bombarded by false teachings, empty philosophies, and legalistic principles. Paul once again reminds them that Christ is all they need. In the next few verses Paul goes on to tell the Colossians how Christ has already completed their salvation. He uses circumcision as the symbol by which to compare their old sinful nature with their new self in Christ. Circumcision was a Jewish ritual that took place the 8th day of a baby boy's life. This was to be an outward sign that this particular child was a part of the Jewish community of faith. God originally intended this to be an act for the Israelites to perform, in order for them to be different from the pagan tribes around them. Christ's work on the cross made these legalistic rites no longer necessary to gain salvation. Salvation was no longer a set of rules, animal sacrifices, and priestly go-betweens. Christ was enough. Now what is important is an inner circumcision of the heart. The false teachers were trying to teach once again that circumcision was required for salvation, and Paul is coming against that with guns blazing. He says circumcision of the heart is all that is necessary and that is done THROUGH Christ—not with the hands of men but through the nail-pierced hands of Christ.

Paul then uses the example of baptism to finish his point. Baptism is an outward expression of our faith in Jesus Christ. It does not determine salvation, but it does testify where we place our trust. It signifies dying to your old life as you go under the water and rising again to a new life in Christ when you come out of the water. Again, it is not a ritual that saves us; it is placing our faith in the person of Jesus Christ that brings salvation.

Paul continues to write about salvation, but goes on to remind the Colossian people of the extent of the debt Christ paid on our behalf. Verses 13 through 15 speak of the written code that was nailed to the cross along with our sins. The false teachers had the Colossians looking back over their shoulders, thinking they constantly had to DO something to earn their salvation, and Paul takes the opportunity here to refute the false teachings of works-based faith.

What is the danger in accepting the false teachings of works-based faith?

_____
_____
_____

Do these verses say that we had to do anything to be made alive in Christ?

_____
_____
_____

What were we before we were alive in Christ? (vs 13)

_____
_____

Do we have to "fix" everything in our lives before we accept His gift of salvation or does He want to save you just the way you are? Explain.

_____
_____
_____

So often we are the ones who complicate faith. Paul taught the simple gospel of grace. We are the ones who think grace is too easy. Just like the false teachers of the Colossian days, we too try to make it way too difficult. The simple truth is that Jesus died so that our sins could be forgiven. The only thing we have to do is accept the free gift of forgiveness. That is it. That is enough. Verse 11 of our text in *The Message* says: *"Entering into this fullness is not something you figure out or achieve. It's not a matter of being circumcised or keeping a long list of laws. No, you're already in—insiders—not through some secretive initiation rite but rather through what Christ has already gone through for you, destroying the power of sin."*

The devil, our enemy, cannot wield his power over you unless you allow it. He and all his powers and authorities were made a spectacle of when Jesus Christ went to the cross. The enemy was defeated. What a reassuring thought that is. You are free if you choose to be free. We are no longer in bondage to the enemy. We were rescued through the blood of Christ.

Have you accepted the free gift of salvation? If so, write down where, when, and how you came to salvation. Include any other information of your salvation experience that you think is necessary to tell your story of grace. This is called your testimony of faith. *(If you cannot answer yes to this question but you would like to accept Christ's free gift, please stop now and pray with someone who can lead you in a prayer of salvation. Or, simply follow the ABC's: pray and A—Accept Him as your Savior, B—Believe that He died, was buried, and rose again on the third day, and C—Confess to Him that you are a sinner in need of forgiveness. It is that simple. If you do this be sure to share it with someone as soon as you can, so you can begin to live out your faith.)*

_____

_____

_____

_____

_____

_____

Paul ends this section of scripture on a victorious note. He states that Christ was triumphant on the cross! He was triumphant, and now we can live in Him. My prayer for you this week is that you too feel triumphant. We have victory over this world because He had the ultimate victory. I pray that you will be rooted in Him, built on Him, strengthened by Him, and thankful because of Him so that you can stand against false philosophies.

In Summary
Now take some time to go through the text once more (Colossians 2:6–15). After studying a little deeper, what did you learn? How can you apply that to your own life?

2:6–7– _____

_____

2:8– _____

_____

2:9–12– _____

_____

2:13–15– _____

_____

Application

In the middle of this lesson we discussed the 4 keys to growth in Christ as Paul outlined in Colossians 2:7. We are going to take our application point from that verse. In *The Message*, Paul says: *"School's out; quit studying the subject and live it!"* Put your books away for today and start living it. Before you return to class next week, write down how you "lived out" the 4 keys to growth in your life. How are you rooted in Christ, built on Christ, strengthened by Christ, and thankful for Him? How are these principles being played out in your everyday life? Do you feel like you are experiencing growth? Explain.

_____
_____
_____
_____
_____
_____
_____
_____

Memory Verse:

"For God was _____ to have all His fullness _____ in Him, and through Him to _____ to Himself all things, whether things on _____ or things in _____, by making _____ through his _____, shed on the _____."

Colossians 1:19–20 (NIV)

Lesson Five

Memory Verse:
"So then, just as you received Christ Jesus as Lord, continue to live in him, rooted and built up in him, strengthened in the faith as you were taught, and overflowing with thankfulness." —Colossians 2:6–7 (NIV)

Read Colossians 2:16–23
Write down your initial thoughts.

_____

_____

_____

Write down any key words you see throughout the text.

_____

_____

In verse 16, Paul once again uses the hinge word: *therefore*. As the old saying goes, we have to find out what the therefore is there for. If you couple it with the preceding verses you will see that Paul is saying: Because Christ did all of this for you, "*do not let anyone judge you by what you eat or drink or with regard to religious observances*" (NIV). There is a connection between the facts of the believer's freedom in Christ to Paul's attack on religious legalism that denied that freedom. The legalism doesn't matter anymore because Christ is enough. His grace is all you need.

Lately I have had the privilege of rereading Having a Mary Heart in a Martha World *by Joanna Weaver. In chapter 4, she spends considerable time talking about the religious rules imposed and developed by the Pharisees in their vain attempt to be a perfect nation. "They took the basic principles that Moses passed on to the Jewish nation and created the Mishnah, a collection of over 600 rules and regulations designed to help Jews live out the Law."*[1] *On the Sabbath it was even unlawful for a man to carry a needle in his cloak because that was considered sewing…hence work. If he dragged a chair across a sandy floor, he was plowing. They even decided it was wrong to eat an egg on the Sabbath because the hen who laid it had been working.*

But instead of drawing the nation of Israel closer to God, the laws became stumbling blocks. It was impossible for the people to carry such tremendous burdens. When Jesus came to earth He immediately began to attack the religious leadership. "Woe to you, because you load people down with burdens they can hardly carry, and you yourselves will not lift one finger to help them" (Luke 11:46, NIV).

Jesus came to remove their burdens and ours as well. "Come unto me, all ye that labor and are heavy laden, and I will give you rest" (Matthew 11:28, KJV). *Jesus knew it was impossible to comply with all of the dos and don'ts that had been so important to the Pharisees. "I have come that they may have life and have it to the full"* (John 10:10, NIV). *He wanted the people to stop focusing on rituals and start focusing on who God really was.*

I believe this is what Paul was trying to help them see—get over all of these man-made rules and regulations. Spend your time getting to know God so you can love and serve Him better. **–Jacki**

Sometimes it is not the religious legalism that keeps us in bondage. Often it is our own set of rules and expectations that holds us captive. It looks different for all of us. Jacki shares her own personal struggle with one thing that holds her back from the freedom she desires:

I have long been a list maker. It has been my security blanket for many, many years. Furthermore, I believe it's my moral obligation to complete everything on the list, regardless of the time and energy it takes! I have taken great pride (oops!) in accomplishing a lot and crossing out item after item on my list as it is completed.

Recently the list has begun to burden me in very much the same way the Mishnah must have been to the Jews. Every day I wake up to "The List," and it has taken some of the joy out of my day. Maybe I am getting old or maybe God is trying to get my attention. Maybe He has some things for me to do that aren't on the list...maybe I am so busy with the list I don't even have time to hear His voice.

It really is a constant battle, isn't it, to balance our activity level. I thought once my girls left home I would be less busy…NOT. Two equal and opposing sayings ring in my ears everyday. The first is: "Whenever possible say yes." The second is: "You can't do every good thing." Both have merit and of course there are times to say "yes," but there are also times when "no" definitely needs to be the answer…without feeling guilty.

If you are a list maker like me, give yourself permission to ignore it for a few days. See if the world ends, or your family collapses, or if your days are filled with more joy, more laughter, and more time to get to know God. **–Jacki**

Jacki brings up a subject that we don't like to discuss…our freedom is most often limited by our own self-imposed list of rules and regulations. Sure, there are times when others expect way too much, or they judge us harshly based on their view of life and Christianity and what it should look like. We should not let other's opinions of us, however, set the expectations, boundaries, or limitations in our lives. Our relationship with Jesus should be the only determining factor in how we live. As your relationship with Him grows, so will your sensitivity to His still small voice. As you listen to Him, study His Word, and live out your faith, He will reveal to you areas of your life that need to be turned over to Him. You will begin to make natural changes in your life based on His leadership and prompting.

His prompting can come through other believers to us. We all need those people in our lives to hold us accountable, as we have talked about in a previous lesson, but be careful that these people are connected to Christ in a very real way. Test any advice you are given by the Word of God. And always temper the choices you make by not only asking, "Is this good for me?" Also ask yourself, "Will this cause others to stumble?" Remember, you are the picture of Christ the world sees. There is a difference in wanting to please the Lord and wanting to please people.

What are some of the *dos and don'ts* by which Christians today sometimes judge each other's faith?

_____
_____
_____
_____

What do the following verses say about whom you should or should not listen to?

Hebrews 2:1–

_____

_____

_____

Jeremiah 23:16–

_____

_____

_____

Matthew 7:15–

_____

_____

_____

2 Peter 2:1–

_____

_____

_____

In verses 16–19, Paul is telling the Colossian people not to give in to the need for the approval of others. Paul tells them that these false teachers have lost touch with the "head" which is Christ. He knows that it takes much more than just following a set of rules and regulations to be protected from falling or giving in to sinful desires. It is about being connected to the head—CHRIST—who enables us to grow beyond and above our sensual desires.

In verse 17, Paul calls these rituals a "shadow." What do you think Paul means when he uses the word "shadow" to describe these things?

_____
_____
_____

What (or who) is reality according to verse 17?

_____
_____
_____

Deeper Still

Using your additional resources, look up what some of these ancient religious rituals or rites were. You can look up the traditional Jewish rituals, religious ceremonies, or even the list of rules that the Pharisees imposed on the people of the day.

_____
_____
_____

Paul refers to Christ with two different descriptors in these verses. He refers to Christ as the reality and the head. Paul gets rather sarcastic when he begins to talk about these false teachers who have not only lost touch with the reality, but have also completely lost their heads! I don't think he uses this tone out of disrespect but rather out of the need to help the Colossian people see the ridiculous nature of legalism.

How does Paul describe these people who are trying to judge the Colossian people (vs 18–19)?

_____
_____
_____

One way he describes them is "having lost touch with the head, which is Christ." How does their disconnection from Christ as their spiritual head help explain the false beliefs of these misguided teachers?

_____
_____
_____

Do you believe we have false teachers today? If so, how are they impacting our world?

_____
_____
_____

We must honor Christ as our reality in spite of the false teachers in the world today. Christ must be the "head" of our lives. How do you honor Christ as "head" in your daily spiritual journey?

_____
_____
_____

How does His "headship" affect your relationships with others? How does this affect your role in the church you attend?

_____
_____
_____

Once you understand the need for Christ to be the head of your life everything else will begin to fall in place. Paul goes on in verse 20 to bring the reader full circle back to the simple fact that Christ died so we could be free. And then he asks a question that I will also ask you:

Why, as though you still belong to the world, do you want to submit to the rules it has placed on your Christianity? Why do we still feel pressured to succumb to opinions that are based on human commands and teachings?

_____

_____

_____

The Word of God is the "plumb line" by which we should live our lives. As Christians we are free from living by human rules, yet we must also honor Christ in our bodies. Our nature is to engage in sin. We have a natural bent in that direction. Paul knew that and wanted the readers to understand that false humility, worldly regulations, and harsh treatment of the body would never be able to curb our appetite for sin. He goes on in Chapter 3 of Colossians to help them see what will help, but at the end of Chapter 2 his focus is to shake them out of the grip of these false teachers by discrediting their arguments, vaccinating them against the poison of their teachings.

What truths have you read in the book of Colossians, thus far, that would vaccinate you and others against the harmful, but often appealing, alternative ways to God and holiness that abound in our world today?

_____

_____

_____

As you read the book of Colossians and study the nuggets of truth within, it is vitally important that you make note of those points that directly relate to you in a real way. The Word of God is active and alive. It is just as true today as it was yesterday, and it will forever be filled with life-giving words of hope for every believer. The key point that Paul continually makes throughout his letter to the Colossian church is the supremacy of Christ. In today's portion of Scripture, he asks them to flee from those that would teach the outward expression of faith over the inward confession of faith…false humility over true sacrifice. I pray that you have felt God tugging at your heart. I pray that you have stepped outside the box of public opinion and self-imposed ritual to a newfound freedom in Christ.

In Summary
Now take some time to go through the text once more (Colossians 2:16–23). After studying a little deeper, what did you learn? How can you apply that to your own life?

2:16–17– _____

_____

2:18–19– _____

_____

2:20–23– _____

_____

Application
Examine your lifestyle, spiritual practices, and attitudes toward other believers. Has this week's study raised any red flags? Spend some time in prayer, asking God to reveal any judgmental attitudes, anything you need to let go of, anything that is in the way of Christ being the head of your life. Ask Him to walk with you daily, keeping you alert to false teachers who would lead you astray. Write down what you feel the Lord is saying to you today. Now spend some time in thanksgiving, by writing a prayer. Do this by putting one of the following portions of Scripture from Psalms in your own words: Psalm 33, Psalm 34, Psalm 92, Psalm 100, Psalm 103 or Psalm 145.

Memory Verse:

"So then, just as you _____ Christ Jesus as _____,

continue to _____ in him, _____ and

_____ _____ in him, _____ in the faith as

you were taught, and overflowing with _____."

Colossians 2:_____

[1] Joanna Weaver, *Having a Mary Heart in a Martha World*, (Colorado Springs: Random House, 2000), 51-52

Lesson Six

Memory Verse:
"And whatever you do, whether in word or deed, do it all in the name of the Lord Jesus, giving thanks to God the Father through Him."
—Colossians 3:17 (NIV)

Read Colossians 3:1–17
Write down your initial thoughts.

_____

_____

_____

Write down any key words you see throughout the text.

_____

_____

_____

Wow, what an amazing passage of Scripture! Have you ever heard the acronym for BIBLE—**B**asic **I**nstruction **B**efore **L**eaving **E**arth? Well, here you have it—doesn't get much clearer than verses 1-17 on how God expects us to live. It is reminiscent of Micah 6:8 (NIV), *"And what does the Lord require of you? To act justly and to love mercy and to walk humbly with your God."*

In 2006, a horrific van accident took the lives of five young people from Taylor University. For five weeks Don and Susie Ryn thought their daughter was alive, but sadly she had died in the accident. The young woman they thought was their daughter—the one they had prayed over and protected during those weeks in the hospital—was actually Whitney Cerak. Whitney was another young woman from Taylor who was in the van during the accident. The hospital had mistaken her for the Van Ryn's daughter. Both the Cerek family and the Van Ryn family profess Jesus as their Lord and Savior, and they went on to co-write the book *Mistaken Identity,* which describes their ordeal. Their story brought national attention to what it means to live a holy life. Their actions and attitudes were very different from the "normal" reactions to mistakes, misinformation, and tragedy. The verse above from

Micah 6 was quoted by Don Van Ryn when asked by the media why his family held no bitterness—why they had not filed a lawsuit regarding the misidentification of their daughter.

Literally millions of lives have been affected by the testimonies of these two Godly families. The host from a national TV program continues to follow their story. He always talks about the profound effect their Christian testimony has had on his life. That's what Paul is talking about in this passage. Our lives should be different; our attitudes should be different because our minds are set *"on things above, where Christ is seated at the right hand of God"* (Colossians 3:1, NIV).

How are you different than your "old self" (before you had a personal relationship with Christ)?

_____

_____

_____

What do you think it means to *"set your minds on things above?"*

_____

_____

_____

In your opinion, what is the difference between being heavenly minded and earthly minded?

_____

_____

_____

In verses 1 and 2, the verbs Paul uses literally mean to "keep on seeking" or "keep on setting" your minds on things above. He is talking about an everyday, all-day-long act of setting our minds well above the earthly realm. It implies that it is an act of persistence, one of determination…to keep on seeking those things.

How do you think we are able to *"set our minds on things above"* or in other words, how are we able to be heavenly minded?

_____

_____

_____

We are able to set our minds on heavenly things because we are with Christ in God the Father. Within that relationship we have the strength we need to keep our hearts longing for what truly matters. We have the will to keep on keeping on.

What do you think it means to be hidden with Christ in God?

_____

_____

_____

An analogy that helps me to picture being hidden with Christ in God is that of a letter in an envelope: When we turn to God for salvation, He puts us in Him right along with Christ; whatever happened to Him happens to us; where He went, we go; where He will be, we will be. Through the cross, death, resurrection and glory, we are placed with Christ in God the Father, just as a letter is placed in an envelope. And, we will be with Him when He returns. Now He, our life, is our body in heaven, and we are His body here on earth. **—Alice**

When Paul uses the word "hidden," he is using the language of Psalms and Isaiah to reflect the safety of God's people in Him.

How do the following verses describe the safety we can have in God, as His people?

Isaiah 49:2–

_____

_____

_____

Lesson 6

Psalm 27:5–6–

_____
_____
_____

Psalm 31:19–20–

_____
_____
_____

God desires to see His people assured and safe in the knowledge that He loves them and is preparing a place for them beyond the grave. And because of this reality, He desires for us to live a life free from our old, sinful, earthly nature. Paul changes his thought pattern to that line of thinking in verse 5. Notice the use of the word *"therefore."* He wants us to understand that, as followers of Christ, who are with Christ in God, we now must be mindful of the way we live. This is much different from the legalism of the false teachers, in that we should live differently because we are ALREADY in Christ, not because we are trying to EARN that position. Because we are in Christ, the things that belong to our earthly nature should no longer be a part of us.

What does Paul say we are to do with our earthly nature?

_____
_____
_____

What things does Paul say belong to our earthly nature (vs 5)?

_____
_____
_____

Paul lists these things, then he reminds the Colossians that they are in their past because they no longer live that life. That was part of their old life.

Moving forward they should not only *"put to death"* the sexual sins he listed here, but also *"rid"* themselves of social sin.

What are the sins that were part of our old selves listed in verses 8 and 9?

_____

_____

What effects do all of the sins listed in verses 5, 8, and 9 have on our relationship with God and others?

_____

_____

_____

Paul challenges the readers to "rid" themselves of sin. This can also be translated as "lay aside" or "put off," and is the same word used when Paul urges believers to lay aside the sins and attitudes that kept them from living freely and fully for Christ in Hebrews 12:1. He is calling for a decisive and immediate break with the ungodly ways of our pasts. He knows that we cannot eliminate the sinful nature as long as we are in this body, but the cross has broken its power over us. Paul has already warned against self-effort and trying to overcome sinful desires by regulations. So then, that begs the question:

How can we, who are sinful by nature, receive the power to overcome sin? Look up the following verses for help:

Romans 8:6–8–

_____

_____

_____

Romans 8:12-14–

_____

_____

_____

2 Corinthians 3:17–18–

_____
_____
_____

Galatians 5:16–18–

_____
_____
_____

Galatians 5:22–25–

_____
_____
_____

Colossians 1:11–

_____
_____
_____

Our power is from the Spirit of God dwelling in us, giving us the strength that we need to be overcomers. But we tend to have problems with that thought, and we give in. Our unbelief gets the best of us, allowing our old sinful, earthly nature to take over, and we go back to doing whatever we want whenever we feel like it. Paul warns the people that they should not be doing whatever they feel like or as *The Message* says, whatever *"attracts their fancy"* (Colossians 3:5, *The Message*).

He recalls for them the fact that they are new and continually being *"renewed in knowledge."*

Think about your life. Is your old life dead? Can people see a difference in your new life? Explain.

_____
_____

How does Paul describe the new self that believers are given in and through Christ? (Refer to verses 3:12–17)

_____

_____

_____

In verse 11, Paul begins to describe in detail for the Colossians that it does not matter what level of society you might find yourself on, we are all created in God's image. Christ is enough for everyone; even if your old self is the lowest of the low, Christ is ALL you need.

What an amazing statement. He follows that thought when he says that we are *"God's chosen people, holy and dearly loved."* Holy literally means to be set apart. Do you feel holy and dearly loved? You should, because as His child, you are!

Now take a look at what Paul says about being this chosen people, about being holy and dearly loved. He begins by once again using that hinge word he loves to use: *therefore*. Since we are new and have let go of our old selves, and since we are *"God's chosen people,"* it is time to clothe ourselves with some new duds!

The NIV Bible puts it this way: *"As one takes off dirty clothes and puts on clean ones, so the Christian is called upon to renounce his evil ways and live in accordance with the rule of Christ's kingdom."*

What do the following scriptures have to say about this?

Galatians 3:27–

_____

_____

_____

Psalm 45:3–

_____

_____

Romans 13:14–

_____

_____

_____

Describe a time when you put on a new outfit or wore formal attire to a black-tie event. How does that experience help you relate to the above verses?

_____

_____

_____

Putting on our new self is not unlike putting on new clothes in the literal sense of getting dressed. Paul lists the virtues that are to be a part of our new self in verses 12 through 17. We make the choice to wear these virtues or leave them hanging in our closet as we engage the world we live in.

Read Colossians 3:12–17 and list the virtues Paul says we are to clothe ourselves with.

_____

_____

_____

Deeper Still
Look up the definitions of each of these virtues individually. As you define them, also use your reference tools to find other scriptures that list these virtues.

_____

_____

_____

_____

_____

Do you ever have trouble *"putting on"* any of these virtues? Explain.

I would have to say that the hardest virtue for most of us to put on is probably forgiveness. We have an overwhelming need to be right, and an overwhelming need for things to be fair. When we feel like someone is in the wrong, or unfairness is in the air, forgiveness is the last thing on our minds. First, we want to see wrong righted and fairness reigning supreme. We can very easily make a mountain out of a molehill. We must choose our battles wisely and always be willing to forgive as we were forgiven our sins. Keep in mind that you can forgive someone without allowing them the control to hurt you again, and you may have to take the journey of forgiveness slowly depending on the circumstances. But bitterness will creep in if we hold grudges, and peace will be something we can only long for and will never find. Paul recognizes that there will be disagreements among believers. The phrase *"rule in your hearts"* gives the image of an umpire arbitrating disputes. He doesn't expect them to be swept under the rug but instead arbitrated in a peaceful manner until, whether in agreement or not, peace can rule. Unity comes from the love we have for one another, and that love is not based on whether or not we agree on everything. That love is based on Christ. Unity should spring from there.

How can you put this idea of love, forgiveness, peace, and unity to practice in your home? In your church? With others?

_____

_____

_____

_____

All of these virtues are difficult to put into practice without the strength of Jesus Christ on our side. Getting up everyday, putting on your new self, and leaving the old self behind takes effort.

Do you remember the song *New Attitude* by Patti LaBelle? This whole point of putting on your new self reminds me so much of that song. Think about what you were like before Christ, or what you are like when you feel disconnected from Him. This is a lesson in comparison and contrast!

Take a few minutes to be honest about who you are when Christ is not in control, then compare who you are when He is in the drivers' seat! Record in the space below your old self versus your new self…your old attitudes versus your new attitudes!

Old Self ─────────────────────────────────────── **New Self**

So many lessons are learned along our journey of life. I learned many of those lessons after I chose to leave my new self behind and carry with me instead my old self with its sinful nature. We could all use an attitude adjustment once in a while because sometimes the wires between our old self and our new self get crossed. That happens to the best of us, but when all of these virtues are working together through the conduit of love within the body of Christ, we can help each other when that happens.

Love has been described as the expression of our connectedness to the God of Life—by whom, for whom, through whom—all things exist. It is God's life-giving attitude of wanting the greatest good for all and asking what positive thing can be done in all situations. Love is what we put on over all other virtues. It is like the overcoat that keeps the other virtues safe and close to our hearts even in the coldest winters of the soul.

When we put love on and wear it over everything else, Christ is exalted. Verses 15 through 17 are the ultimate marching orders to do just that. In *The Message* it says: *"Let every detail in your lives—words, actions, whatever—be done in the name of the Master, Jesus, thanking God the Father every step of the way."*

What do you think it means to do something *"in the name of the Lord Jesus?"*

_____

_____

_____

_____

If I do something in the name of someone, I am doing it in his or her stead. I am representing them. Paul tells the reader that whatever they do, in word or deed, they should do it in the name of Jesus.

How does this change the way you do things?

_____

_____

_____

_____

Paul ends this inspiring section of his letter with a request to give thanks. This should come as no surprise. He sounds like a broken record: thankfulness, thankfulness, thankfulness.

Why do you think Paul sees thanksgiving as such a vital role in the life of the believer?

_____

_____

_____

Giving thanks to God for what He has given me helps me remember why I should then do my part to live as His ambassador to a lost and dying world. It gives me strength to do whatever I do in His name. I pray that His sacrifice and your acceptance of that sacrifice, brings about new changes in your life. I pray that you are never the same. I pray that as you experience the fullness of Christ, you will find that He is enough to help you daily put on your new self and continually leave your old self behind. But, most of all I pray that *"whatever you do, whether in word or deed, [you will] do it all in the name of the Lord Jesus."*

In Summary
Now take some time to go through the text once more (Colossians 3:1–17). After studying a little deeper, what did you learn? How can you apply that to your own life?

3:1–4– _____

_____

3:5–7– _____

_____

3:8–11– _____

_____

3:12–15– _____

_____

3:16–17– _____

_____

Application
This week choose 2 or 3 of your daily activities at home, work, or play. Do each one intentionally with Jesus, thinking how He would see and do them. Keep thanking Him in your heart. Then record below how this conscious partnership affected you and what you did differently.

_____

_____

_____

_____

_____

_____

_____

_____

_____

_____

_____

_____

_____

_____

Memory Verse:

"And _____ you do, whether in _____ or

_____, do it all in the name of the _____

_____, giving _____ to God the

_____ through Him."

Colossians 3:17 (NIV)

Notes:

Lesson Seven

Memory Verse:
"Whatever you do, work at it with all your heart, as working for the Lord, not for men." —Colossians 3:23 (NIV1984)

Read Colossians 3:18—4:1
Write down your initial thoughts.

_____
_____
_____

Write down any key words you see throughout the text.

_____
_____
_____

In addition to our text this week, read Ephesians 5:22—6:9 then write down any additional thoughts you might have about the subject matter of these two similar portions of Scripture.

_____
_____
_____

This portion of Scripture is all about relationships. If you are not married or if you are not a parent, please don't check out or skip this lesson. The Word of God has much to say about how to maintain healthy relationships. And this is a very direct portion of Scripture regarding how we should act in relationship with others. When thinking about studying the Word of God, don't just think about it in terms of how it will help you. Having an intimate knowledge of the Word of God will not only help you, it will also help you minister to others.

Can you think of a time when studying God's Word helped you to be an encouragement to someone else? Explain.

_____

_____

_____

Undoubtedly, we have all been in a position where we are helping someone we love through a difficult situation. Whether it is a marital issue, a physical illness, rebellious children, a stressful work situation, or any number of other situations, we all have had to walk one or more of these roads beside a friend or family member. Whoever you are, whatever season of life you are in, this part of Paul's letter is for all of us. We all can learn something from his words of instruction on relationships.

The first relationship Paul addresses is that between a husband and wife. He uses a word in the first verse that causes many women to stop dead in their tracks. On the contrary, many men love that Paul uses this word.

What is this controversial word that Paul uses in verse 18? What is it that Paul says wives should do?

_____

_____

_____

What do you think the word "submit" means?

_____

_____

_____

Much has been written and debated about this verse. What does the word "submit" really mean? In *The Message* they translate this word as *"understand and support your husband."* New Century Version says, *"yield to the authority of your husband."* This word does most often speak of obedience, but here the word says the wife is to show respect to her husband as an act of submission to the Lord. Whatever phrase or word you choose, the bottom line is one of respect. Wives should respect their husbands. A husband does have an incredibly difficult role to play in a marriage. Not only does he have a spiritual responsibility, he also carries the tremendous responsibility of providing financially for his family. Even in today's society when so many women work outside of the home, men still believe it is ultimately their responsibility. And even the most outwardly secure man believes he could lose his job at any time. Imagine the weight that idea carries. Men can carry whatever burden is given them as long as they feel respected. In general, a man would rather live life alone than to feel he is inadequate or disrespected.

For married women only:
1. For the next week do not criticize your husband…about anything. See if you have fallen into a pattern of criticism that may be chipping away at his self-esteem. Next week, tell your group how you did.

2. What are some ways you and/or your family can honor your husband this week?

_____

_____

_____

_____

If you are not married:
1. For the next week do your best to live a life of respect for those around you. Maybe this is at work or in another relationship. See if you have fallen into the critical spirit trap. Next week, tell your group how you did.

2. What are some ways that you can honor those you have friendships and/or relationships with this week?

_____

_____

_____

_____

For men only:

1. What do you feel the respect level in your home is? If you are not married, what is the respect level in your most valued relationships?

_____
_____
_____
_____
_____

2. How does this make you feel?

_____
_____
_____

Paul knew that relationships are two-sided. So, he does not let the husbands off the hook. It is not just about respect, it is about love too. In verse 19 he shows that this is not a one-sided submission but a reciprocal relationship of love. Just as respect is the primary need for men, love is the primary need for women.

For married men only:

1. For the next week, demonstrate your love to your wife in ways she would not expect. (These do not need to be expensive. It is the thought behind the love that counts.) Next week, tell the group how you did.

2. What are some ways you and/or your family can honor your wife this week?

_____
_____
_____
_____
_____

If you are not married:

1. For the next week, demonstrate your love for others in ways they would not expect. (These do not need to be expensive. It is the thought behind the love that counts.) Next week, tell the group how you did.

2. What are some ways you can improve in showing love to those you come in contact with everyday?

_____
_____
_____

For women only:

1. What is the love level in your home? If you are not married, what is the love level in your most valued relationships?

2. How does that make you feel?

_____
_____
_____
_____
_____
_____

These questions could possibly open up painful discussions. Be sure to approach this subject with mercy, love, and grace for one another. Remember, God's Word is available to us for growth and change. No one is perfect. We all have room to grow. There is no room for big egos inside healthy relationships. Be willing to listen and do your best to apply what you learn from His Word to your marriage, friendships, and other relationships in your life. Perhaps you have been disrespectful or unloving without even knowing it, and in the process you might have hurt someone important to you. If that is the case, own it, learn from it, and do your best to change!

If you are the one who has been hurt or disrespected in some way, be willing to forgive. Give grace to your offender and be sure to give respect and love when you have a desire to get respect and love in return. Do not attack. Accept the fact that we all fail and do things we don't mean to do. Do what you can to earn respect, and give love to those around you, understanding that growth within relationships is a process. It will take time to get it right. In fact, you will find most often that relationships are not perfect or right. They are worth the work you have to put into them, which adds value to the relationships you have had the longest. Work hard to build relationships that offer a safe place for each of you to be who you really are.

Paul now turns his attention from the marital relationship to the relationship between children and their parents. In verses 20 and 21, he speaks in a very direct manner about not only the necessary obedience of children, but also the responsibility of parents, both mother and father, to act appropriately toward their children. Paul tells parents that they must surrender the right to act unreasonably toward their children. If you are not a parent, this section can be helpful in your relationships with your nieces and nephews, friend's children, or in your future parental role.

Wherever we are on the parenting spectrum, we want our children to be obedient. But we need to be in tune with the heart of our children in order to discipline them correctly. What is effective and appropriate for one child may be ineffective and inappropriate for another. Each child is made unique and special.

(**If you are not a parent**: as you read through the following questions, answer them from either the perspective of a child, a future parent, an observer of others' parenting skills, or one that has a significant role to play in the life of a child.)

Do you think you can parent or discipline every child the same exact way? Explain.

_____
_____
_____
_____
_____

Share a time when you thought yours or another's use of discipline had effective results.

_____

_____

_____

Share a time when you thought those disciplining skills totally missed the mark.

_____

_____

_____

What did you learn from each experience?

_____

_____

_____

What do you think it means to act unreasonably toward your children?

_____

_____

_____

_____

Parenting is a job that takes one person way beyond themselves into a world where the well-being of this little one MUST come before his or her own well-being. It is a calling that is most gratifying and most frustrating all at once. Parenting is both rewarding and draining. Sometimes we become a parental figure in the lives of children that are not our own flesh and blood, but need parenting just the same. Kids today need guidance, direction, and unconditional love. They live in a world that is pulling them in every direction except the right one, and a healthy relationship with a mentor, whether a parent or another adult, is a necessity. When a child lives in a home where the parents act unreasonably toward their children, many times rebellion or withdrawal become symptoms of the deep need they have to be loved. That same rebellion and withdrawal can become symptoms of the deep need that ALL of us have to be loved when we are embittered or provoked by someone with whom we are in a close relationship.

If you look closely at the teaching of Paul in this section you can see that he is encouraging a set of distinctive attitudes that are necessary in any healthy relationship. In his instruction to parents he is impressing on them to act reasonably. In his instruction to wives he stresses respect, and to husbands …love. Reasonable behavior, respect, and love are all attitudes that are necessary to live in harmony with others.

Are these attitudes distinctive in your own life and relationships? Explain.

_____

_____

_____

Do you need to work on any of these attitudes? Explain.

_____

_____

_____

Paul continues to encourage the Colossians in right attitudes in Colossians 3:22 through Colossians 4:1. But, in doing so he brings up a sensitive subject…slavery. "The Bible does not expressly condone or forbid slavery. In the New Testament, Jesus heals a slave and commends his owner for his faith. He does not take the time to condemn the slave owner for having a slave, nor at any point does he try to suggest that slavery is wrong. Saint Paul said this to slave owners: 'Do not threaten [your slaves], since you know that he who is both their Master and yours is in heaven, and there is no favoritism with him' (Ephesians 6:9, NIV). The Old Testament goes a little further and reminds people to treat their slaves well. The most likely reason for this apparent moral discrepancy is that the Bible was penned at a time when slavery was not only widespread, but considered perfectly normal and moral—there was no reason to mention it as most people wouldn't have considered it an issue worth thinking about. Slaves at the time were generally treated much better than the slaves of modern times and would usually end up being made free after a number of years of servitude."[1]

Deeper Still
Look up further history on slavery during biblical times versus modern day slavery. Write down what you find.

_____
_____
_____
_____
_____
_____

Instead of focusing on this issue that is obviously a modern day travesty and one that scars the history of our country, let's go deeper into the message of this section of Paul's letter. Beyond slavery, this section is about having a good work ethic. And it gives us step-by-step instructions on how to develop and maintain a good work ethic. I love the section that says: *"keep in mind always that the ultimate Master you're serving is Christ."* Paul is making the same point here that he was making back in Colossians 3:17 & 23 when he says: *"Whatever you do, whether in word or deed, do it all in the name of the Lord Jesus, giving thanks to God the Father through Him."* This is a work ethic that goes far beyond us and enters the realm of remembering who it is we represent.

Many years ago I was employed in a full time position. For financial reasons my hours were cut from 40 hours a week to 32 per week. I was surprised and very angry. While I could have totally justified someone else's hours being cut, I simply could not or would not justify it when it was my own. So I went to work angry and bitter for the next 2 days, barely speaking to anyone. The weekend came and I was still stomping around, complaining about the unfairness of it all. Fortunately I have a Godly husband, and he kindly reminded me that I had a choice—I could either be a light in a dark world or I could just be the dark world. Ouch! After prayer and reflection I asked God to forgive me for my terrible attitude. When I walked into work on Monday I greeted everyone with a smile, asked about their weekend and went about my work...with a pleasant attitude. Later that day my boss told me she had been holding her breath, waiting for me to come in on Monday, hoping against all hope that I would no longer be angry. She said, "I can't tell you how relieved I was to hear your voice and know the storm had passed. I need to know you are okay so I can be okay and do my job." Our attitudes in the work place, wherever that is, affect everyone. Is your light shining or hidden under a bushel like mine was? —**Jacki**

I would venture to say that until recently most Americans viewed their job as a right instead of a privilege. And, just like Jacki, they can find themselves in a major attitude funk when things are not going their way. Today we understand all too well that having a job is most definitely a privilege we should not take for granted. Yet, there are those that still work with the wrong attitudes.

Part of the process of having a good work ethic is to understand the difference between a right and a privilege. How would you define the difference?

_____
_____
_____

How would you describe a good work ethic?

_____
_____
_____

Is there someone, past or present that has shown you what good work ethic looks like? Explain.

_____
_____
_____

So often we fall into the trap of "I will treat you how you treat me." Paul is asking the Colossian people and us not to fall into that trap. In our work ethic we are to exemplify Christ. In our relationships, we are to exemplify Christ. In our parenting, we are to exemplify Christ. In our marriages, we are to exemplify Christ. We are to act reasonably, respecting and loving those around us no matter how they may treat us. In essence, Paul is calling us to LIVE OUT OUR FAITH … our faith in Christ. And Christ is enough to help us do just that!

In Summary
Now take some time to go through the text once more (Colossians 3:18—4:1). After studying a little deeper, what did you learn? How can you apply that to your own life?

3:18–19–

_____

_____

_____

3:20–21–

_____

_____

_____

3:22—4:1–

_____

_____

_____

Application

This week examine your attitudes. Try your best to open yourself up to the people in your life you are closest to. Ask them to hold you accountable to the attitudes that Paul challenged us with this week: acting reasonably, respectful, loving, and demonstrating a good work ethic. Write down any ways that you might have struggled or any insight you gain by intentionally looking for these in your own life.

_____

_____

_____

_____

_____

Memory Verse:

"Whatever you _____, work at it with _____ your _____,

as working for the _____, not for _____..."

Colossians 3:23 (NIV1984)

[1] (http://listverse.com/2009/01/14/10-fascinating-facts-about-slavery/. The Bible and Slavery).

Lesson Eight

Memory Verse:
"Devote yourselves to prayer, being watchful and thankful."
—Colossians 4:2 (NIV)

Read Colossians 4:2–18
Write down your initial thoughts.

_____
_____
_____

Write down any key words you see throughout the text.

_____
_____
_____

Paul begins this portion of Scripture with the familiar subject of prayer. He doesn't just ask the Colossian people to pray. He asks them to *"Devote themselves to prayer."*

What do you think it means to *"Devote yourself to prayer"*?

_____
_____
_____

Now, look up the definition of "devote." Write down the definition in the space provided.

_____
_____
_____

Do you think that you personally have a devotion to prayer? Explain.

_____
_____
_____

What steps can you begin taking to protect your personal prayer life in order to grow in your personal devotion to Christ?

_____
_____
_____

What do the following scriptures have to say about the devotion Jesus had to prayer?

Luke 5:16—

_____
_____
_____

Matthew 14:23—

_____
_____
_____

Mark 1:35—

_____
_____
_____

In *Walking with the Savior*, Max Lucado says this about prayer: "Father, when you were on earth you prayed. You prayed in the morning, you prayed at night, you prayed alone, you prayed with people. In your hours of distress you retreated into times of prayer. In your hours of joy you lifted your heart and hands to the Father in prayer. Help us to be more like you in this way... help us to make prayer a priority in our daily lives."[1]

In times of stress (both good stress and bad stress) do you naturally go to God in prayer? Why or why not?

_____

_____

_____

What do you think the purpose of prayer is?

_____

_____

_____

Prayer is the number one way to tame a worry habit. Joseph M. Scriven's hymn says it all: *"O what peace we often forfeit, O what needless pain we bear, All because we do not carry everything to God in prayer."*

Paul says in Philippians 4:6 (NIV 1984), *"Do not be anxious about anything, but in everything, by prayer and petition, with thanksgiving, present your requests to God."* He wanted us to understand in Philippians and now again in Colossians that prayer is a key aspect of our walk with Christ. In Colossians 4:2, he couples prayer with being watchful and thankful. Being watchful and thankful are like the two legs of prayer. They help to keep us balanced in our prayer life. A watchful individual is alert, attentive, and perceptive to what is going on around them and also ever listening for the still small voice of God when He is speaking. A thankful individual is well aware of the blessings in his or her life, keeping him or her focused on the good and from being anxious or worried.

Look up the following verses and list the things that we are to be alert and watchful for:
Matthew 26:41–

_____
_____
_____

1 Timothy 4:16–

_____
_____
_____

1 Peter 5:8–9–

_____
_____
_____

Deeper Still
Look up the following scriptures and record how they relate to being watchful in prayer: Luke 10:38–42, Deuteronomy 18:15; 30:20, Proverbs 1:5, and James 1:19.

_____
_____
_____

Thanksgiving has been described as the outward expression of inner gratitude.
What are some reasons believers have to be thankful to God, according to the following scriptures?
Psalm 30:11–12–

_____
_____
_____

Psalm 107:20–22–

_____

_____

_____

Colossians 1:3–4–

_____

_____

_____

Colossians 1:12–

_____

_____

_____

1 Thessalonians 5:18–

_____

_____

_____

Paul not only asks the Colossians to be devoted to prayer for themselves, but in verse 3 he also asks them to pray for him and those serving with him in carrying the message of Christ to the nations. He feels a deep responsibility to make sure the message is spread, and that it is done so in a way the people he is ministering to are able to understand and relate to the message. He is passionate about the message being spread across the world as he knew it. In verses 5 and 6, he urges the Colossians to be just as passionate as he was about making Christ known to all.

Paul asks the Colossian people to *"make the most of every opportunity."* What do you think this means?

_____

_____

_____

Where do you come in contact with unbelievers? How can you make the most of those opportunities in pointing them to Christ?

_____

_____

_____

Verses 5 and 6 go hand in hand. Paul continues to speak of how we are to behave when we are with people who do not have a personal relationship with Christ. He says to *"make the most of every opportunity,"* to *"fill your conversations with grace,"* and to be *"seasoned with salt so that you may know how to answer everyone."*

Look up the meaning to the word "grace" or "gracious." Write down the definitions here.

_____

_____

_____

_____

What do you think it means to *"fill your conversations with grace"*? Why should an attitude of grace always permeate all of our conversations?

_____

_____

_____

Paul also says to be *"seasoned with salt."* One commentary says that this means to not be insipid, dull, or full of Christian clichés. It means that your conversations should be "tasteful" just as salt seasons food and makes it palatable...flavorful for those you are speaking to. So too, your conversations should have a sweet aroma to God the Father.

Knowing what it means to season our conversations with salt, how does this mean we are to talk with unbelievers about our faith or other things?

_____

_____

_____

At the end of his letter in verses 2-6, Paul wants to make sure we understand just what it means to live our lives before unbelievers in a way that would lead them to Christ. Then he goes on in verses 7-18 to introduce the readers to the men serving alongside him in reaching the unbelievers they came in contact with. The first impression of this last section of chapter 4 is that we all bring different gifts to the table just like Paul's partners in ministry. Tychicus was a faithful minister and servant. Onesimus was part of the church at Colossae; Aristarchus sent his greetings as did Mark and Justus who were fellow Jews working for the kingdom. Epaphras, also from Colossae, was a prayer warrior, and Luke was a doctor and disciple. They were all gifted differently, but they still worked as a unit to spread the truth of Jesus Christ. No one gets an "excused absence." We are to be about the work of bringing others to the foot of the cross. God can use every one of us in our own unique way to minister to and reach the lost. Some of us may be at home, praying "without ceasing" to undergird other believers who may be going into uncertain and perhaps unsafe environments to spread the love of Jesus.

What do you feel like your role or gift is in leading people to Christ?

_____

_____

_____

Has God called you to a ministry that you need to carry out and com-

plete? Explain.

_____
_____
_____

Paul was doing ministry beside many individuals, but there was one in particular who is worth noting just for learning's sake. Mark was listed in verse 10. This is important because the Bible tells us that Paul did not take Mark on his 2nd missionary journey because Mark had "deserted" him at Pamphylia (see Acts 15:38). Yet 12 years later they seem to have resolved their issues and are working together. Paul was willing to mend fences with Mark for the sake of the ministry. He sets an example in word and in deed. If Paul had held a grudge there would have been people that would have not heard the gospel.

What about you? Are you holding a grudge against someone that is keeping you from experiencing what God has in store for you? Explain.

_____
_____
_____

From Mark, Paul continues talking of his fellow ministers in verse 12. He speaks very highly of one minster in particular, Epaphras.

How would you describe Epaphras from what you learned in Colossians 1:7 and now in Colossians 4:12–13?

_____
_____
_____

Compare the things Epaphras prayed about with Paul's prayer in Colossians 1:9–12. Write down what you find.

_____

_____

_____

How do their prayers reflect their concern over the situation in the Colossian church?

_____

_____

_____

Epaphras was not shooting quick arrow prayers up to God. He was *wrestling*, this is the verb *agonizo* from which the English *agonize* is derived. It was used primarily as an athletic term. Paul used the same word of himself in verse 1:29. The word is sometimes translated as *"strive"* and *"fight."*

What things might Epaphras be wrestling with and fighting against as he intercedes for the Colossians?

_____

_____

_____

Just as Epaphras wrestled for the Colossian people in prayer, we also have times where we find ourselves wrestling in prayer over personal, urgent concerns. Having others pray with us always brings a renewed source of strength as we wait for the Lord. Paul felt the same way. He found strength in serving and praying with other ministers. And, he made a habit of affirming those who served with him.

Lesson 8

What part do you think Paul's habit of affirming others played in multiplying his efforts and in uniting the scattered churches?

_____
_____
_____

Do you make a habit of affirming the people around you? Explain.

_____
_____
_____

Do you make a habit of affirming those that serve in ministry around you? Explain.

_____
_____
_____

Paul took his responsibilities seriously. He not only felt responsible for spreading the gospel, he also felt responsible to uplift others spreading the gospel. He knew that Christ was all that the world needed to be saved, and his greatest desire was to see the news spread far and wide. After reading and studying the book of Colossians, our prayer is that you would also have an overwhelming desire to see the gospel message spread. If he truly is enough for you and everything you encounter in life ... then share the good news! Spread it far and wide—JESUS IS ENOUGH! HE IS EVERYTHING!

In Summary

Now take some time to go through the text once more (Colossians 4:2–18). After studying a little deeper, what did you learn? How can you apply that to your own life?

4:2–4– _____
_____

4:5–6– _____
_____

4:7–9– _____
_____

4:10–18– _____
_____

Application

This week take on the responsibility of affirming someone serving in ministry. This could be a pastor at a local church, a missionary in the mission field, someone who volunteers time to do ministry of any kind, or even someone who has personally ministered to you in some way. Whoever it is, make an effort this week to thank them for spreading the good news of the Gospel of Jesus Christ.

_____
_____
_____
_____
_____
_____

Memory Verse:

"Devote yourselves to _____, being _____ and _____."

Colossians 4:2 (NIV)

[1] Max Lucado, *Walking with the Savior* (Wheaton: Tyndale, 1996) 102.

Notes:

Lesson Nine

Christ is...Enough
A FINAL GREETING

Memory Verse:
"He is always wrestling in prayer for you, that you may stand firm in all the will of God, mature and fully assured." —Colossians 4:12 (NIV)

This Bible study is intended to be an encouragement toward growth and application. Paul would have been extremely disappointed if the Colossian people had read his letter, put it back in the envelope, and gone about their business as usual, never giving his words a second thought. That would have been a lost effort. Instead, Paul meant for his letter to cause them to move beyond their complacency and to get down to the business of growing in their faith and spreading the Gospel of Christ.

In the same fashion, our heart's desire is that you would begin to see growth in your life every time you are in His Word. Because of that desire, we have all written you a final greeting, a look into what we have gained while writing this study. I pray you will receive a very visual picture of the heart God has given us for you, and a real glance at how we are applying the Word of God to our lives. **Your assignment for next week follows our letters.**

Studying Colossians was a challenge for me in many ways, but as with most challenges, I am glad I went through it. For me, the applications I took from this letter were mostly about my thinking, not my outward behavior. A verse I quote to myself frequently is part of Luke 6:45. In the translation I remember, it's "Out of the overflow of the heart, the mouth speaks." I use it to remind myself not only that what I hear from others reveals to me what they are thinking, but also that what I say reveals to others what I am thinking. So I think this verse tells me, mainly, to watch my mouth.

But through Colossians, I see the verse pointing to my heart first. Does my heart believe that Jesus is all I need? If my heart believes it, my mouth will speak of my confidence, my assurance. In this way, Paul is a great example. His words reveal his heart. He DOES know that Christ is ALL. And Paul's words DO spill over from that cemented confidence. His heart is also overflowing with genuine concern for the people he loved who were in danger. If his heart had been indifferent, his words would have reflected it, but they did not. His words reveal his pure motives and solid faith. —**Erin**

I've been thinking about the word "enough." What does enough *really* mean in our daily lives? Have there been times in my life when God and God alone was enough? Can I think of a specific time when God being enough defied logic? As I contemplated these questions I was reminded of a devotional I wrote a few years ago when we were studying Proverbs. Here's an excerpt from that devotion:

> "One of the questions in our lesson was, 'Who is the friend who is always with you? **How is He the perfect friend?**' The answer of course is Jesus. There will be a day when Jesus is all you have. It will be just you, your circumstance, and the Lord. If that hasn't happened to you yet, you just haven't lived long enough. But I want you to understand that you do not need to be afraid of that day. In Deuteronomy 31:8 we read, 'The Lord himself goes before you. He will never leave you or forsake you. Do not be afraid.'"

The day I was diagnosed with cancer I was completely alone. I was in Ann Arbor at a specialist and had foolishly turned down offers from several friends to go with me. I wasn't trying to be cavalier; I just did not get the seriousness of the situation.

As the day progressed it became more and more obvious to me that the news was going to be grim. I remember vividly sitting in the exam room, clutching my Kleenex® and being overwhelmed with my circumstance. But almost immediately I knew that I needed to pray. I said, "Dear Lord I have been foolish. I'm here by myself, and I need your help. Please be with me in a mighty way in the hours ahead. Give me courage to hear the doctor's words and help me understand what he is saying. I thank you for being Lord of my life, and I am trusting in you. Amen."

I grabbed a new Kleenex® and within minutes the doctor did indeed tell me that I had a cancerous tumor. It knocked the breath out of me, but I was also overcome with an incredible peace. I heard and processed everything the doctor said and even asked good and relevant questions.

At the time I understood that the peace came from God, but it wasn't until this lesson that I understood He was not only all I had but He was all I needed. He was the perfect friend. What a perfect opportunity for Him to show me that God and God alone can carry us through the biggest storms of life.

Friends, that's what it means to be "enough." God is enough to meet all your spiritual needs and God is enough to meet all of your daily stressful life needs. In fact He is more than enough! May God continue to bless your spiritual journey. **—Jacki**

The Letter to the Colossians put me where I so needed to be and so longed to be: in Christ. I was struggling to hold on to my sense of God's presence in a world where people are indifferent to God, take pride in self-directed lives, live divided against each other and their own souls, and practice injustice and hatred in the name of religion. And I know that I too am prone to the pride and selfishness that blocks the love of God.

Colossians shone the light that I sought; it is saturated with Christ. Almost every verse reveals something about Jesus Christ and how all life and history are about God expressing Himself in Jesus Christ. I had learned these truths separately, but seeing them all together in Colossians was a spotlight on Christ that radiated His glory.

Paul gives me the corrective glasses that I need to keep beholding the invisible Christ in this troubled world: set your heart and your mind on the things of the heavenly realm, where Christ is (Colossians 3:1-4). How radical the Christian life is! Contrary to how I appear or feel, the Source of my life is in another Person and another World. I am freed from self-concern and worries when I see my life, other people, and events from the perspective of my loving Savior and Friend who is always working out His life-giving purpose. I don't have to explain why bad things happen to good people; knowing the divine purpose of God in Christ (1:15-20), I believe that every event that happens, good and bad, is an opportunity for man to realize that the life of our souls doesn't come from anything in this temporal, visible world, but from the invisible, eternal Triune God.

Paul's teaching reminded me of a concept that A.W. Tozer wrote about. Basically he noted that it does make a difference here on earth if we see ourselves as a spiritual being. It would also make a difference in the way that I live if I see myself as separate from Christ or IN Christ. Paul clearly writes that living for Christ is a continual choosing—everyday we have to make the choice of putting on our old self or putting on Christ. It is the mindset of doing everything in the name of Christ, not in our own names (Colossians 3:17).

I sometimes want God to make that choice automatically for me. I want to be a spiritual giant like Paul. But love is a choice. Every time I choose to act for Jesus in obedience, my roots draw from Him and I experience His love and power for me. Then receiving His grace in my weakness fills me with gratitude and a joy overflows.

Colossians also reminded me how completely other-centered the love of Christ is. The incarnation and cross prove how universal His passion is for people to know Him and to be reconciled into union with God, the maker of their soul. If I am going to love other people as Christ Jesus loved me, I must give my body and time as He did to being His messenger of hope and light. Every person that I see during my day is a person of great interest to Jesus and should be to me too. In Chapter 4, Paul calls us to stay alert, to pray, and to look for ways to work with Christ in our interactions with unbelievers.

Paul's final greetings are a great example of his teaching on the interdependence of the members of Christ's body and our need to work together in humility and love. The four of us had an opportunity to exercise that interdependence as we developed this study guide. I had to focus on doing my part, and only my part, as I relied on Christ to teach me. It has been wonderful to see Him living and working in the lives and hearts of Crystal, Erin, and Jacki.

It is my desire and prayer that Christ Jesus will use the Letter to the Colossians to transform your view of Him, of yourself, and of the world. Live upward for "Christ in you, the hope of glory." —**Alice**

In the midst of this study I found myself going through some interesting things in my personal life. One situation was that our oldest son broke his collarbone in February and had to have surgery to put in a plate to stabilize the bone. In April we were still in the middle of the recovery stage, and our son was struggling with the aftereffects of the injury. As a mother, I found it hard to see my son struggle; I just wanted to fix it for him instead of spending hours worrying and fretting over the smallest things. Colossians hit me straight in the face with the fact that I could never do enough to fix everything for my child or myself for that matter.

Paul spoke directly to me when he said, "Let the peace of Christ rule in your hearts, since as members of one body you were called to peace. And be thankful" (Colossians 3:15, NIV).

I had been dwelling in a perpetual state of fear and worry. I had so much to be thankful for, yet I was focused on the negative...the "what ifs." Colossians challenged me to change my focus and trust once again in the powerful strength of Christ. He is enough for me, for my children, and for everyone. That knowledge takes so much pressure off of me. I don't have to play God, because He IS God!

I hope you have found the peace that passes all understanding...the peace that you can only find in relationship with Christ. It takes surrender on your part. Allowing Him to be your all-in-all means you have to take a back seat and LET Him! He can be your satisfaction, your hope, your joy, your peace, and so much more. The study of Colossians reminded me of many things I had forgotten or chosen to ignore. Now that I have been reminded, I am doing my best to apply the truth I have seen, in a new way, through the eyes of Paul.

My prayer is that the Book of Colossians has permeated your heart with truth that you are now applying to your walk. Jesus is ENOUGH for whatever you are going through. I can tell you from experience. I believe the Lord God knew I needed to study Colossians, because He knew I would need it for that season of my life. I have officially been reminded and will do my best to always remember...Christ does not need my help...HE IS ENOUGH! **—Crystal**

Your Assignment

What about you? What has God been saying to you through the book of Colossians? It is your turn. **Write your own final greeting...a letter expressing what you have learned and how you plan on applying it to your everyday life. The letters you write will be part of your last class together.** I hope you will enjoy hearing what God is doing in the lives of those you have walked this journey with! (If you are doing this study alone, your letter will be something you can look back on to see how God was at work in your life. I think you will find it an encouragement to you when the doubts come.)

"Grace be with you."

Memory Verse:

"He is always _____ in _____ for you,

that you may stand _____ in all the will of _____,

_____ and fully _____."

Colossians 4:12 (NIV)

Lesson 9

Appendix A -
RESOURCES

CONCORDANCES
- *Bible Concordances*, (Pocket Series), NKJV, Thomas Nelson Publishers, 1999.
- *NIV Compact Concordances*, Zondervan Publishers, 1993.
- *Strong's NIV Exhaustive Concordance*, Zondervan Publishers, 1989.

DICTIONARIES
- *Nelson's New Illustrated Bible Dictionary and Concordance*, Thomas Nelson Publishers, 1995.
- *New Bible Dictionary*, Second Edition, Inter-Varsity Press, Downers Grove, IL, 1994.
- *The New Combined Bible Dictionary and Concordance*, Baker Book House, 1996.
- *NIV Compact Dictionary of the Bible*, Zondervan Publishers.
- *VINE'S Concise Dictionary of the Bible*, Thomas Nelson Publishers, 2005 (Gives access to Greek and Hebrew words).

COMMENTARIES
- *Believer's Bible Commentary*, Thomas Nelson Publishers, 1989.
- *Halley's Bible Handbook*, Zondervan Publishers, various editions.
- *New Bible Commentary*, 21st Century Edition, Inter-Varsity Press, 1994.
- A variety of commentaries are available and useful for single books of the Bible.

ON-LINE RESOURCES
- bible.crosswalk.com
- biblegateway.com
- biblia.com
- biblestudytools.com
- ewordtoday.com
- gotquestions.org

BIBLE READING PLANS

- Schedules for reading through the Bible are available at Christian bookstores and sometimes included in a Bible. Some of the websites listed above under ON-LINE RESOURCES offer various plans and tips for Bible reading. See Zondervan.com for reading plans that you can customize and print out.

Appendix B -
MEMORY VERSES

Below are suggested memory verses, which express a truth or principle of each week's lesson text. These are only suggestions. If there is a different verse that God uses to enlighten you, memorizing it will help you to remember what you have learned. The importance of memorizing Scripture can't be exaggerated. If we put it in our minds and treasure it in our hearts, the Holy Spirit can help us recall it as we need it, bringing the light of God's Presence and Truth to our situations. Some of the memory verses are in the New International Version (NIV), and some are from *The Message* translation. Use other versions if you prefer.

Lesson 1
Colossians 1:13–14 – "God rescued us from dead-end alleys and dark dungeons. He's set us up in the kingdom of the Son he loves so much, the Son who got us out of the pit we were in, got rid of the sins we were doomed to keep repeating." (*The Message*)

Lesson 2
Colossians 1:16–17 – "For by him all things were created: things in heaven and on earth, visible and invisible, whether thrones or powers or rulers or authorities; all things were created by him and for him. He is before all things, and in him all things hold together." (ESV)

Lesson 3
Colossians 1:27 - "The mystery in a nutshell is just this: Christ is in you, so therefore you can look forward to sharing in God's glory. It's that simple. That is the substance of our Message." (*The Message*)

Lesson 4
Colossians 1:19–20 – "For God was pleased to have all his fullness dwell in him, and through him to reconcile to himself all things, wheth-

er things on earth or things in heaven, by making peace through his blood, shed on the cross." (NIV)

Lesson 5
Colossians 2:6–7 – "So then, just as you received Christ Jesus as Lord, continue to live in him, rooted and built up in him, strengthened in the faith as you were taught, and overflowing with thankfulness." (NIV)

Lesson 6
Colossians 3:17 – "And whatever you do, whether in word or deed, do it all in the name of the Lord Jesus, giving thanks to God the Father through him." (NIV)

Lesson 7
Colossians 3:23 – "Whatever you do, work at it with all your heart, as working for the Lord, and not for men." (NIV 1984)

Lesson 8
Colossians 4:2 – "Devote yourselves to prayer, being watchful and thankful." (NIV)

Lesson 9
Colossians 4:12 – "He is always wrestling in prayer for you, that you may stand firm in all the will of God, mature and fully assured." (NIV)

BIBLIOGRAPHY

Bradbury, William. "*The Solid Rock*" Lyrics, Edward Mote, 1837.

Halley, Henry H. *Halley's Bible Handbook*. Grand Rapids: Zondervan, 1961.

http://listverse.com/2009/01/14/10-fascinating-facts-about-slavery/

Lucado, Max, *Walking with the Savior*. Wheaton: Tyndale, 1996.

Scriven, Joseph M. "*What a Friend We Have in Jesus*" 1855.

Tomlin, Chris; Giglio, Louie, "Enough"©2002 worshptogether.com Songs (ASCAP) sixsteps Music (ASCAP) (adm. at CapitolCMGPublishing.com) All rights reserved. Used by permission.

Van Ryn, Don; Susie Van Ryn, Newell Cerak, Colleen Cerak. *Mistaken Identity: Two Families, One Survivor, Unwavering Hope*. New York: Howard Books, 1st Edition, 2008.

Weaver, Jcanna, *Having a Mary Heart in a Martha World*. NEW YORK: Random House, 2000.

CPSIA information can be obtained
at www.ICGtesting.com
Printed in the USA
FFOW05n1552230815